TEACHERS' GUIDE TO DESIGNING CLASSROOM SOFTWARE

TEACHERS' GUIDE TO DESIGNING CLASSROOM SOFTWARE

JULIE M.T. CHAN
MARILYN KOROSTOFF

SAGE PUBLICATIONS
Beverly Hills   London   New Delhi

For information address:

SAGE Publications, Inc.
275 South Beverly Drive
Beverly Hills, California 90212

SAGE Publications India Pvt. Ltd.
C-236 Defence Colony
New Delhi 110 024, India

SAGE Publications Ltd
28 Banner Street
London EC1Y 8QE, England

Printed in the United States of America

Library of Congress Cataloging in Publication Data

Chan, Julie M. T.
    Teacher's guide to designing classroom software.

    Bibliography: p.
    1. Computer-assisted instruction—Programming.
I. Korostoff, Marilyn. II. Title.
LB1028.65.C48 1984   371.3'9445   84-6962
ISBN 0-8039-2313-9

FIRST PRINTING

CONTENTS

Introduction

- Why You Should Read This Book
- What This Book Is About
- How You Can Use This Book
- What You Will Learn
- How This Book Is Unique
- Our Philosophy Regarding Computers in Education

This book is written for teachers who want to design their own educational software programs, but who are not sure how to begin. The easiest type of educational software for beginners to design is the Computer Assisted Instruction type of program. CAI programs are widely used and are most helpful to students. These programs provide for greater time on task in order for students to practice skills that require initial exposure; consequently, it might be a good idea for you to begin with a CAI type of program. Then, as you become more proficient at designing educational software or *courseware,* you can "graduate" to designing more creative and complex programs such as simulation, problem solving, modeling, or demonstration type programs.

WHY YOU SHOULD READ THIS BOOK

There's something for everyone in this book . . .

If you are a teacher who is just beginning to use computers, this book will serve as a guide to selecting quality educational software programs. You will learn what features to look for, why they are important, and how they work.

If you are a teacher who is using computers with purchased "off-the-shelf software," but are not always able to find the exact courseware that you need for your instructional objectives, this book will tell you how to design your own.

If you are an educator who has recently acquired programming skills and are now eager to "conquer the world" with programs that are waiting to be written, this book will serve as a guide to designing the courseware, refining your writing, and helping you produce a professional product.

If you are an educator or a computer programmer who has been writing educational software for some time, this book will provide you with techniques to refine your craft. If you are a programmer who is not also an educator, this book contains suggestions that are based on sound principles of teaching and learning that will make your courseware pedagogically more effective.

If you are a student majoring in education, this book will not only help you design educational courseware, it will also show you how to apply the theories of teaching and learning that you have been studying in your methods courses.

WHAT THIS BOOK IS ABOUT

This book is about designing the best possible educational software given the technology that is available at this time, so that you will be able to use the computer to enhance your teaching and so that your students will be able to learn most subjects more quickly and easily in an enjoyable manner.

Chapter 1 involves preliminary planning that requires you to make important choices before you roll up your sleeves and get down to work. Careful planning is the key to creating educational software programs that will be both effective and useful.

Chapter 2 helps you structure the content of your program by showing you how to construct a task analysis, determine benchmark learnings, establish criterion frames, and write the objectives for the program.

After that brief introduction, Chapter 3 is designed to be used as a workbook of step-by-step instructions. It shows you how to develop and use each of the seventeen program modules in the Courseware Design Framework. The modules provide the framework or skeleton upon which to build a courseware program for initial teaching (tutorial), review and reinforcement, or drill-and-practice. The extent to which each module is used will determine whether the final product is a tutorial, review and reinforcement, or drill-and-practice program.

Seventeen modules came to be included in the framework as a result of much time spent in previewing, reviewing, and evaluating educational courseware. We felt that many educational software programs could be strengthened or enhanced if certain elements were included. The seventeen modules constitute an "ideal" program — there is yet to be any one program the authors have looked at that contains all seventeen elements! However, a program can still be of good quality without containing every one of the seventeen elements. But if all of the elements were included in one form or another, the program would be a well thought-out program design.

Chapter 4 contains a sample lesson that illustrates the modules and concepts discussed in Chapter 3.

Chapter 5 discusses techniques for programming your educational software. It contains alternatives on what to do if you are not proficient at computer programming.

Chapter 6 discusses how to evaluate your courseware; several sample evaluation forms are included.

Chapter 7 contains ideas for marketing and selling your completed educational software product. A directory of companies that are developing and marketing educational software will help you decide how to look for a company to help you sell your new product.

The bibliography contains further readings on the topic of software development. Since this is a practical "how to do it" book, much of the educational theory behind program design is not dealt with in this volume. Instead, some of the references provide excellent discussions on program design theory.

HOW YOU CAN USE THIS BOOK

Of course, you can start at the beginning and read through to the end, becoming familiar with how to design educational software along the way. You may also skim through the book until you find a specific area that is of particular interest to you. Following are some guidelines that may help you decide how you can use this book most effectively.

WHAT TO DO BEFORE YOU BEGIN

Before you read this book, decide what *type* of educational software you want to write, *how* you will use it, and *why* you are taking the time (and effort) to write it. If you have spent some time reviewing some of the educational programs that are on the market, you will have a better idea of what most educational software is like. Once you have that background, the ideas discussed in this book will make more sense and the suggested techniques for improving what is currently on the market will be apparent.

WHICH PARTS OF THIS BOOK SHOULD YOU READ?

This book is designed so you can use it whichever way makes the most sense for you, depending on your level of expertise in designing and programming educational software. Each of the sections begins with an overview, followed by a detailed explanation of each concept. Read the chapter overview to determine whether you are interested in or need to read that section.

WHAT YOU WILL LEARN

When you are finished reading this book, you will know how to design a program for educational purposes and be able to construct a task analysis to determine the scope and sequence of the content to be contained in your program. You will be able to recognize the features in quality educational programs and you will have a fundamental idea of the parts of a sound educational program. You will be able to talk to computer programmers and let them know what you want in a program that will help you effectively teach or enable students to practice a given skill or concept. This book will *not* make you an expert programmer, but it will help you become a better educational software purchaser and/or program designer so you can fully exploit the features and potential of the computer.

As an experienced teacher, you are a curriculum specialist in the subject area(s) you teach. Thus, you are in the best position to also design educational courseware since you know *how* students learn — as well as *what* they need to learn . For these reasons, you should become involved in designing educational courseware even if you don't know how to write computer programs. You can always team up with a professional programmer once the design is in place. The design of a program is critical to its effectiveness for students and its usefulness to teachers. Only *you* can do that.

HOW THIS BOOK IS UNIQUE

Although there are other books on how to design educational software, this book is unique in that the Courseware Design Framework is based on the mastery learning model created by Dr. Madeline Hunter of UCLA. All of the effective teaching/learning principles we have used and practiced as successful teachers in the classroom are incorporated in the Courseware Design Framework—from constructing a task analysis for the content items at the beginning to the closure at the end of the courseware.

Sample criterion-referenced pre- and posttests are included to provide examples of how to design easy and accurate placement tests at the proper level of learning and for determining the content, concepts, or skills to be practiced. Specific practice and/or test items are earmarked as *benchmark* or *criterion* items to indicate mastery or understanding of the concept or skill being studied.

Another unique feature is that the scope and sequence is based on Bloom's Taxonomy of the Cognitive Domain, which orders items from simple to complex in terms of levels of thinking. Items are coded through an item analysis so that a prescription with follow-up activities can be built in.

The courseware should be coordinated with other teaching materials so that teachers can make use of instructional materials they already have in their classroom. In addition, this courseware coordination makes it easier for teachers to integrate the use of computers into all areas of the curriculum effectively.

OUR PHILOSOPHY REGARDING COMPUTERS IN EDUCATION

We believe that the human element is crucial in the teaching/learning process. The teacher is the curriculum specialist and is the person most knowledgeable about how students learn. Their education, experience, and expertise can never be replicated by a computer. Therefore, we feel that *the computer can never replace the teacher.* However, the computer can be harnessed to make the teacher's job more effective. It can free teachers to concentrate on the one thing they do best—teaching—and providing the guidance and warm encouragement that only a human being can give!

Computer courseware should be used in the same manner that educational films are used in the classroom. For example, before a film is shown to students, teachers normally (1) preview the film, (2) plan for its use in a purposeful manner as a tool to supplement, augment, or enrich their teaching, (3) make sure it promotes the instructional objective(s), (4) provide students with a purpose for viewing the film by giving them points to look for, and (5) follow up the viewing with a discussion or other meaningful activity to get the most out of the time invested viewing the film. These same steps should be applied to using educational software programs.

1 Preliminary Planning

- Identification Data
- Content
- The Student Population
- Program Technique
- Content Structure
- Physical Design
- Presentation Formats
- Evaluation
- Collateral Instructional Materials
- Courseware Coordination

It is important to think through carefully what you will write for use on the computer before you begin its actual design. That way, you will know exactly *what* you are producing and *how* you will use it. This section of the book forces you to make some important choices before you actually roll up your sleeves and get down to work designing a piece of educational courseware. *Careful planning* is the key to creating a program that will be both effective and useful. The following sections should be given careful consideration before you begin the actual courseware design process.

IDENTIFICATION DATA

In this section, include the following information: (1) your name, (2) the starting date, (3) the completion date, and (4) the approximate hours it took you to work on the project. Although it is not necessary to do item four, keeping track of how long it takes you to write a program will enable you to estimate more accurately the time it will take you to work on future projects.

CONTENT

SUBJECT AND CONTENT AREA

Decide on the subject or content teaching area. Subjects such as reading, language arts, math, science, and social studies are popular. Now that computer literacy is becoming a subject for study, this could be yet another content area (and one for which there are relatively few teaching materials).

TOPIC OR SKILL

Within each subject, there are specific topics and/or skills to be mastered. Courseware that teaches a transferable skill and fits in with most academic subjects will be very popular.

INSTRUCTIONAL OBJECTIVE

The objective of your program should be clearly stated at the *beginning* of any collateral material, such as a study guide or teacher's manual, for the convenience of potential users such as teachers and parents. In addition, the objective should be stated in the courseware program itself so students will be made aware of what they are learning, why they are learning it, and how it will be useful to them. If an objective for a program cannot be defined or expressed in one or two sentences, then it may not have been clearly thought through by the courseware designer and needs to be rewritten.

THE STUDENT POPULATION

GRADE LEVEL(S)

The grade level(s) should be clearly identified in the written literature *and* on the disk label. Programs that claim to be appropriate for grades kindergarten through 12 are generally useless because no single teaching material could possibly be "all things to all learners."

ABILITY LEVEL(S)

The ability level should also be specified because one group of third-grade students who are identified as gifted would be very different from another group of third graders who are remedial. Thus, ability level must be kept in mind when designing (and selecting) appropriate courseware.

LEARNING STYLE(S)

Learners can interact with the computer through several channels: visual, auditory, and kinesthetic. Because of this multisensory aspect of computer learning, children with different learning styles can find computers equally beneficial.

PROGRAM TECHNIQUE

There are three main ways that educational courseware is being used in today's classroom: (1) Computer Assisted Instruction, (2) Computer Enriched Instruction, and (3) Computer Managed Instruction. These three ways are also referred to as *program techniques*. Within each of the three techniques, there are further subcategories, called *program functions*. In the paragraphs below, the program functions for each of the three main techniques will be explained.

COMPUTER ASSISTED INSTRUCTION

Programs that are used to teach, reteach, review, or provide for drill and practice after a skill or concept has been previously taught are referred to as computer assisted instruction or CAI software. Tutorial type programs are used to teach a skill "from scratch" and are useful for capable students who are able to learn advanced concepts on their own. Programs that are designed to *reteach, review,* or *reinforce* are useful for students who need a second "go around" on a concept or learning, for students who were absent when the concept was initially presented by the teacher, or for students who need to be retaught a particular skill or concept. Students who need more practice or additional "time on a task" in order to master it benefit from courseware that is of the *drill-and-practice* function. Of all educational courseware sold in 1983, 75% fall into the CAI category. Of this, 90% of all CAI programs were drill-and-practice in nature.

COMPUTER ENRICHED INSTRUCTION

Courseware in this category enables teachers to enrich and enhance their classroom instruction. The three primary functions under CEI include simulations, modeling, and problem solving. In *simulation* programs, the computer is used to "imitate real life situations" and the user becomes the main character or actor in control of the situation. *Modeling* programs enable users to try out or test ideas. For example, in redesigning a school cafeteria, an architect can use a computer to determine the best floor plan for handling a maximum traffic flow during peak use hours. Students can experience the process of *problem solving* because situations can be easily posed on the computer and, in order to be successful, students must (1) define the problem, (2) develop a plan, (3) carry it out, and (4) evaluate it.

COMPUTER MANAGED INSTRUCTION

Computers can also be used to assist teachers in routine classroom management tasks such as test preparation, administration, and scoring; using test results on which to base additional instruction; and other routine tasks such as record keeping, attendance, scheduling, and so on. Although this category of software does not directly affect students per se, computers can reduce the time spent on time-consuming routine administrative tasks and free the teachers for more time to work directly with students.

CONTENT STRUCTURE

Content can be approached in various ways on a computer. For example, an idea can be presented in its simplest form and built upon until it becomes fully developed. Or, it can start with simple examples that can later be generalized. Finally, it can start with a general concept that is then applied to many examples. Any of these approaches may be used in designing your courseware, but the final decision will depend on the nature of the content, the skill being presented, and the ability level of the learners.

PHYSICAL DESIGN

There are five physical designs for educational courseware: (1) linear designs, (2) spiral designs, (3) branching designs, (4) multitrack designs, and (5) regenerative designs.

LINEAR DESIGN

Linear design courseware takes all learners through a program from start to finish using the same set of items in the same sequence regardless of ability. Although it may take some students longer than others to complete a program, all students must do all of the items in the same sequence. This design does not provide for much flexibility in learning, nor does it make use of the computer's ability to branch.

SPIRAL DESIGN

Spiral design courseware takes a given concept or idea and applies it to many situations. For example, in a study of the circulatory system in science, the basic concept is first presented. Then the circulatory system of various species of animals are explored so the learner will be able to generalize how the circulatory systems are similar or different among various animals. Another example is the study of people's homes. Once the concept for a dwelling is presented, the homes of people in various geographical areas, climates, and cultures are studied. Among the generalizations that a student may discover are that homes are more alike than different, that the materials used to build a home is dependent on the raw materials available in the immediate area, and that the design of a home is dependent on its function and the lifestyle of the people who live in it.

BRANCHING DESIGN

One of the advantages of a computer is its ability to branch. Depending on the choice a learner makes, the computer will accommodate that selection by branching elsewhere in the program and amplify that concept. The computer can allow the items to become increasingly difficult, in small increments, thus enabling the learner to experience success. Concepts can then proceed from simple to complex through branching.

MULTITRACK DESIGN

An effective program accommodates learners at their ability level. Levels of learning may be determined in several ways: (1) from the results of a placement test (which is part of the program or on paper), (2) the students' choice of difficulty level at which they chose to work, or (3) determined by the student's rate of success in a lesson. The multitrack design allows programmers to build more than one level of difficulty into a program.

REGENERATIVE DESIGN

Programs that have a regenerative design allow teachers to use the program more than once. For example, spelling programs and vocabulary practice programs are often of the regenerative design so teachers may reuse these programs by typing in each week's list of spelling or vocabulary words.

PRESENTATION FORMATS

Programs may be presented in one of the following formats: (1) multiple choice, (2) matching, (3) true/false, (4) fill-in answers, or (5) open-ended answers.

MULTIPLE CHOICE

This format is recommended for tutorial and drill-and-practice programs because it structures a learner's response to an item. It is also easier to design the feedback for this format because the choice of answers is controlled by the program designer.

MATCHING

This format is a good one for very young students. For example, primary students can easily match words with pictures.

TRUE/FALSE

Although this format is an option, true/false questions are generally not recommended because students often select correct answers for the wrong reasons, or wrong answers for the right reasons. True/false questions do not enable students to apply fully what they have learned.

FILL-IN ANSWERS

The fill-in format usually requires exact answers. The computer can be programmed to "read" an answer by searching for key letters, even if a word has been misspelled or the phrasing and responses vary from one student to another. Full or partial credit may be given for misspelled words if the program designer chooses.

OPEN-ENDED ANSWERS

The open-ended answer format is the most difficult for the designer because students' responses vary. At this time, computers are not able to make evaluative judgments regarding the quality or correctness of answers. Unless a subject is such that an open-ended answer is the best approach or if it is the only way that a student is able to provide feedback on content mastery, it is not recommended—at least not on a computer!

EVALUATION

You can improve your program through the process of evaluation. Each of the following steps will help you revise and refine the program in order to make it better.

EXECUTION TIME

It is important to determine how long it takes for your program to run because most students are not able to maintain sustained attention on a task for more than 15 minutes. Since computers are still a novelty and since most students do enjoy working on one, they are usually more willing to work on it for more than 15 minutes. However, the day will come when even a computer cannot sustain a student's undivided attention for more than 15 minutes. Therefore, it is important to restrict your program's running time to not more than 10-15 minutes. You may design your program so that students can determine (1) how much time they will spend on the program with a preset timer, (2) how many items they will complete, or (3) by using the exit option if it runs longer than their allotted 15 minutes on the computer and other students are waiting their turns.

TEST RUN

If you choose to write the program yourself, it should be checked out continuously while it is being written to make sure that all of the parts work. Otherwise, if a programmer waits until the entire program is coded in, the number of errors, or "bugs," in the program may be too overwhelming, and, consequently, too frustrating to have to spend so much time trying to take out the errors in order to make it run smoothly. Professional programmers budget about half as much time for debugging their programs. In other words, for every 10 minutes spent writing a program, allow at least 5 minutes for debugging. It may take a person more time to debug when they are new to programming than when they become more experienced.

FIELD TESTING

Programs should be field tested with students similar to those for whom the program is being designed. That way, adjustments may be made before a program becomes widely used. A program should be field tested on individual students, on groups of students, on students who are high in ability as well as those low in ability. As you write your program and test run it, see if you can "crash" it (make it inoperable)—something that some students may try when they use your program!

EVALUATION BY COLLEAGUES

In addition to having students use your program, ask your fellow teachers to try it out. Not only should other teachers try it, but perhaps *their students* should be asked to use it too. If you try out your program with various groups, you have more opportunities to refine the courseware before it goes on the market, when you no longer have control over altering it for any unanticipated problems!

USING COURSEWARE EVALUATION FORMS

Put your program to the "test of fire" by using one of many courseware evaluation forms to see how it measures up. You may also ask teachers to evaluate your program and even students who are old enough to fill out an evaluation form.

COLLATERAL INSTRUCTIONAL MATERIALS

The term "courseware" implies that a computer program is accompanied by instructional materials that will make using that computer courseware more effective. Some of the materials that should be included are (1) a teacher's guide containing (a) a synopsis, summary, or courseware highlights, and (b) lesson objectives, (2) pre- and posttests, (3) lesson plans, (4) overhead transparencies and other visual aids, (5) reproducible student worksheets or workbooks, and (6) additional suggestions for using the program.

TEACHER'S GUIDE

The teacher's guide should include (1) a synoposis, summary, or highlights of the program; (2) all of the frames in the program (along with the full text) so it is not necessary for a previewer to have to sit through the entire program in order to see what it does; and (3) the objectives for the program so the teacher will know what the program's intent is. The program must be designed so it will achieve the stated objectives once a student has finished using your courseware.

PRE- AND POSTTESTS

Students may be tested to determine whether they need additional practice on a specific skill at the computer. Pre- and posttests may be an integral part of the computer courseware, but it is recommended that they also be available in printed form in the event a teacher wishes to administer the test to a group of students in order to save time (and to save space on the disk!). Many programs have a management portion that includes pre- and posttests.

LESSON PLANS

Lesson plans are extremely helpful to busy teachers who want to be able to quickly glance at the objectives, learn what materials are needed, know what kinds of activities are planned, preview the questions, and so on, in order to save time when using the courseware. The lesson plan should also show teachers how to quickly and easily integrate the courseware in with what they may already be doing in other curricula areas.

OVERHEAD TRANSPARENCIES AND OTHER VISUAL AIDS

Visuals enable a teacher to preteach a concept prior to having students go to the computer for further practice. Visuals in the form of masters to be made into transparencies save busy teachers preparation time. The quality of the preteaching presentation can be controlled when a publisher makes and/or provides the visuals.

STUDENT WORKSHEETS

Written materials allow students to follow through a computer-based activity with additional practice (if needed) and further reinforce the skill. Reproducible worksheets that accompany the courseware are a definite convenience for busy teachers. If the worksheets that accompany a program are not entirely suitable, capable teachers will adapt them to fit the students' needs, ability levels, or maturity levels.

ADDITIONAL SUGGESTIONS

Suggestions for further use of the program will enable teachers to use it more than once and in different ways with different students. Programs that can be used in more than one way are more valuable to teachers.

COURSEWARE COORDINATION

Most computer courseware is being used in isolation at this time. To overcome this problem, courseware must be designed as an integral part of a lesson plan that includes preteaching the concept or skill, using the courseware, then following through after its use. For these reasons, computer courseware *must* be used (1) in conjunction with textbooks, library books, or any supplementary texts that are used in the classroom; (2) as part of a unit to augment, supplement, enhance, or enrich the curriculum; (3) with written follow-up or homework assignments; (4) with other visual materials; and, perhaps, (5) with other courseware.

Courseware is more effective when it is used as part of a total teaching/learning sequence—rather than by itself, in isolation. A computer and the programs that run on it should be a means to an end—that of learning a concept or mastering a specific skill—not an end in themselves.

LESSON PLANS

A computer should be as much of a teaching tool as your textbooks, audiovisuals, and other materials. By writing lesson plans that purposefully include the use of the computer, there is less of a tendency to a misuse, abuse, or underuse it. Courseware should be listed under the *materials* section in a lesson plan and it must be on hand for a specific part of the lesson. A word of caution: The program itself may need to be pretaught prior to its use if certain features, such as directions on what to do, are not included in the lesson when the program is run.

COORDINATION WITH OTHER TEACHING MATERIALS

Keep in mind those materials and activities you already use that would comple-ment the courseware. Textbooks, library books, and other teaching materials should be coordinated with the courseware. Courseware use should serve a definite purpose, not just "that the computer is available." Unless the computer can provide a mode of instruction that is not possible with any other teaching tool that teachers or students have at their disposal, it may not be an appropriate use of an expensive piece of equipment. To use the computer as an electronic page turner or electronic workbook is a waste of money. But if certain features and benefits are made possible only by exploiting the computer's potential, then its use may be justified.

Be sure to note the specific textbook and page numbers with which the computer courseware can be used. The courseware should supplement, augment, and enhance whatever else is presented through textbooks, library books, and other teaching ma-terials. Thoughtful planning will make computer use more effective.

COORDINATION WITH EXISTING CURRICULUM

Teaching units, instructional activities, and learning centers can include the use of computers. However, appropriate courseware is critical. Regardless of how the computer is used, it must be *purposefully coordinated* with the existing curriculum—and not regarded as "something extra" or as "frosting on the cake." Computer use must be an integral part of what is already being done.

HOMEWORK ASSIGNMENTS

As more families buy computers for the home, their use for homework assignments will become more commonplace. When computers are widely available, teachers may wish to send work home on a disk; and the completed homework will be returned on another (data) disk. The checking, correcting, and recording of the student's work will be done by computer and stored (on disks) until grades for report cards are prepared. This will be a terrific time-saving device for teachers. It will also help students realize that the computer is an extremely useful tool.

FOLLOW-UP ASSIGNMENTS

Not all students are able to master a concept during its initial presentation. Therefore, provision may be made for students to follow up one computer-based activity with another computer-based activity to reinforce the original activity. Students may also be given follow-up assignments in other learning materials such as textbooks and worksheets on the same skill.

SUGGESTIONS FOR CLASSROOM USE

Courseware authors must provide teachers with many suggestions for practical and creative ways to use the program so teachers will get more mileage out of the program. The ideas should require a minimum of preparation. As the courseware designer, you should be prepared to provide at least a dozen suggestions for ways that your program could be used (1) by students of various abilities, (2) in various subject areas, (3) by students who work alone, who work in pairs, who work in groups, and (4) for suggestions for using your program when only one computer is available and there are 30 kids! It is up to *you* to provide the teacher with highly useful and practical ideas since you are the one who knows the most about your program.

2 Structuring the Content

- Task Analysis
- The Process
- Benchmarks
- Criterion Frames
- Constructing the Task Analysis
- Objectives
- Screen Layout

TASK ANALYSIS

The content of a lesson should be well organized and presented clearly. Organization and clear presentation can be ensured by using a *task analysis approach*. This is the process of determining the major learnings in a specific instructional area and examining all of the component parts or skills needed to master the concept(s). The parts are arranged from simple to complex and then each major learning with its component parts is placed in a sequential format.

THE PROCESS

The process of constructing a task analysis of the content to be taught involves four main steps:

(1) First, *brainstorm* all of the concepts or major learnings needed to master the content area you have chosen.

(2) Next, *eliminate* all of the contaminators. Contaminators are those learnings that are unnecessary, not desired, or those learnings that may hinder or confuse the learner.

(3) Then, *categorize* those learnings or concepts that seem to relate to one another.

(4) Finally, *sequence* the learnings from simple to complex.

BENCHMARKS

After the concepts have been sequenced, write an objective for each learning. It is important to determine exactly what you want to teach on each screen. It is also essential to decide how the students will achieve the objectives. At this time, it may be appropriate to break down the learning even further by determining the component parts. These parts are often called "lead up" skills. It is necessary to master the lead up skills in order to obtain mastery of the main objectives. The task analysis will undoubtedly be composed of several major objectives (sometimes called "benchmarks"), and a series of intermediate skills that lead up to each objective. When constructing a task analysis, it may be helpful to use Bloom's (1962) *Taxonomy of Educational Objectives*. Sequencing the objectives and the skills according to the taxonomy provides for a simple to complex organizational format.

CRITERION FRAMES

As stated above, when your objectives have been written, it is time to actually plan the skills necessary to achieve each objective. Again, a task analysis should be used because every objective will have several lead up skills that are sequenced from simple to complex.

As a method of evaluation, a specific question should be designated, or coded, as the *criterion item*. This question should be the major item that tests for mastery of each objective. Progress can then be monitored according to the mastery of objectives. In addition, the user or instructor will know what concepts need to be retaught or reviewed based on the results of the criterion questions. It is far more efficient to examine the results of the *criterion questions* before prescribing further lessons for the students than to examine all items that are presented or missed.

CONSTRUCTING THE TASK ANALYSIS

Let's imagine that you are designing a lesson to teach students about the various applications of computers. The following is an example of how a task analyis may be constructed for this lesson. First, *brainstorm* a list of as many computer applications as possible:

STEP 1.   BRAINSTORM

Concept: **Computer Applications**

banking functions
creating student programs
calculator
evaluating books
sales projections
use as a typewriter
video games
checkbooks
rocketry
research reports
making decisions
word processing
budget managers
Disneyland rides
preparation of medical
    and legal reports
controlling specific
    operations or processes

pilot training
transportation systems
IRS records
boats
business
financial projections
mailing lists
robotics
help people
billing
teacher's aid
police records
entertainment
math calculations
airline and space flight
    training
cruises
writing books

STEP 2.   ELIMINATE THE CONTAMINATORS

Eliminate all learnings that may not be appropriate or any concepts that you simply may not want students to learn at this time. For example, from the list above, delete the following items: cruises, pilot training, help people, boats, teacher's aid, making decisions, and evaluating books.

STEP 3. CATEGORIZE AND SEQUENCE

From the list generated in the brainstorming, determine the major categories. For example:

(1) Information Storage and Retrieval
(2) Simulations and Modeling
(3) Process Control
(4) Computation
(5) Data Processing
(6) Word Processing

MAJOR CATEGORIES AND SEQUENCED LEARNINGS

Next, group the appropriate learnings under each category:

Information Storage and Retrieval: (1) checkbooks; (2) creating student programs; (3) mailing lists; (4) IRS records; (5) police records.

Simulations and Modeling: (1) entertainment; (2) video games; (3) teaching; (4) airline and space flight training.

Process Control: (1) Disneyland rides; (2) transportation systems; (3) robotics; (4) rocketry.

Computation: (1) calculator; (2) math calculations; (3) math homework.

Data Processing: (1) banking functions; (2) finance; (3) budget managers; (4) billing; (5) sales projections.

Word Processing: (1) used as a typewriter; (2) writing books; (3) research reports; (4) preparation of medical and legal reports.

OBJECTIVES

The next step is to write your objectives based on the categorized and sequenced learnings. The following is a sample of a task analysis of objectives that will teach the concept of computer applications. It is best to begin with an overall objective that will give the lesson a general focus.

OVERALL OBJECTIVE

Students will be able to name six broad areas of computer applications and give examples of how the computer can be used in each area.

LESSON OBJECTIVES

(1) Students will recognize the appropriate information storage and retrieval functions of the computer.

(2) Students will recognize and indicate (by pressing the key for the correct answer) that computers can be used as an information storage and retrieval device.

(3) Students will recognize the appropriate simulation and modeling functions of the computer.

(4) Students will indicate that computers are used as simulation and modeling devices.

(5) Students will recognize the appropriate process control functions of the computer.

(6) Students will indicate that computers are used as process control devices.

(7) Students will recognize the appropriate computation functions of the computer.

(8) Students will indicate that computers are used as devices for computation.

(9) Students will recognize the appropriate data processing functions of the computer.

(10) Students will indicate that computers are used as data processors.

(11) Students will recognize the appropriate word processing functions of the computer.

(12) Students will indicate that computers are used as word processors.

After the task analysis of objectives has been completed, you will be ready to begin designing your educational program.

SCREEN LAYOUT

Every screen in your lesson should follow a predetermined format. That way, students will know *where* to look for (1) the item to be taught, (2) the instructional message telling them what to do, and (3) the feedback after they have responded. It is important to have consistency throughout the lesson to avoid confusion. Whatever organizational format you decide on, be sure to stick to it throughout the entire program.

LABEL

(1) I T E M

(2) INSTRUCTIONAL MESSAGE

(3) F E E D B A C K

—PRESS THE SPACE BAR TO CONTINUE—

3 The Program Modules

- **Overview:** How the Modules Fit Together
- **Module 1:** Identification Data
- **Module 2:** Title
- **Module 3:** Naming/Purpose
- **Module 4:** Pretest
- **Module 5:** Menu
- **Module 6:** Directions
- **Module 7:** Lesson/Content
- **Module 8:** Mini-Tutorial
- **Module 9:** Feedback
- **Module 10:** Coaching
- **Module 11:** Record Keeping
- **Module 12:** Posttest
- **Module 13:** Exit
- **Module 14:** Closure/Review
- **Module 15:** Scoreboard
- **Module 16:** Prescription/Assignment
- **Module 17:** End of Program

OVERVIEW: HOW THE MODULES FIT TOGETHER

A piece of quality educational software should incorporate certain basic elements or modules. By including these modules, consistency, continuity, and completeness will be insured. An explanation and discussion of each module follows.

MODULE 1: IDENTIFICATION DATA

The identification data module provides information about the program. The title, author, programmer, CAI type, subject, skill, date, computer system, and memory requirements should be included so that when a printed copy of your program is made, the reader will have this important information.

MODULE 2: TITLE

The title module will be the first "screenful" of information the user will see. The program title, author, and copyright date go in this section. Graphics, color, sound, and animation should be considered because it will be the users' first exposure to the program and this screen should "grab" their attention. Be sure to give the user the option of turning off the sound, if sound is part of your program.

MODULE 3: NAMING PURPOSE

The computer should ask for the user's name in order to personalize the program and facilitate interaction between the student and the computer. In addition, the user's name can be used throughout the program. Next, the purpose of the program should be explained so the student will have a clear understanding of what is expected.

MODULE 4: PRETEST

The pretest is an optional module in most programs, but is essential in a tutorial type program because it allows the computer to determine the user's learning level in order to "prescribe" the appropriate lesson.

MODULE 5: MENU

The menu is like a table of contents, listing the contents of the program. The user will choose an activity from the menu and work through that part of the program. It is important to include an "exit program" choice in the menu. This allows the student the option of leaving the program as needed.

MODULE 6: DIRECTIONS

The directions module should tell the students exactly what they are to do. It is also important to tell them what they can expect to see on the screen and how they should input their responses. The task may be demonstrated or modeled in this part of the program.

MODULE 7: LESSON/CONTENT

This is where the computer does the actual "teaching." When preparing this section, it is important to refer to the task analysis. Each screenful of information can be a lesson designed to teach each objective.

MODULE 8: MINI-TUTORIAL

A mini-tutorial may appear anywhere in a program. For example, if a student is working along in a program and experiences difficulties, the computer can branch to a mini-tutorial to review or reteach the concept. The student is then able to continue the program on the same concept and may have the items previously missed represented. A mini-tutorial can also be used at the beginning of a drill-and-practice type program to refresh the student's memory in order to prepare the student for the drill-and-practice program. If a student does poorly on a pretest, a mini-tutorial can be presented prior to working on a program.

MODULE 9: FEEDBACK

The feedback module contains comments regarding a user's input or responses to the items in the program. Feedback comments should be positive for correct answers and encouraging for incorrect responses; derogatory comments are not appropriate in an educational environment.

MODULE 10: COACHING

Coaching is a method of providing feedback to students when they get the wrong answer. It assists the learner by giving appropriate clues that lead the student to a correct response. In the mastery learning model, clues are an essential component that facilitate maximal learning of the concept.

MODULE 11: RECORD KEEPING

A program may be coded to keep a record of correct and incorrect responses. The score may be displayed at any time throughout the program or it can appear at the end. Ideally, the program should be designed to keep track of missed items according to each skill or concept contained in the program. This would allow the computer to "prescribe" an appropriate assignment in the homework module based on the types of items missed.

MODULE 12: POSTTEST

Although a posttest module is optional, in a tutorial program it is mandatory. Posttest questions should be constructed to measure the student's performance against the objectives and should contain criterion referenced questions that directly test what was taught.

MODULE 13: EXIT

The exit module allows the student to leave the program at predetermined points. These points can be interspersed throughout the program or can be inserted after the completion of a specific section in the program.

MODULE 14: CLOSURE REVIEW

The closure module focuses the student on the concept and simply tells them what they have just learned. Suggestions regarding applications of this concept to classroom use can be made at this time.

MODULE 15: SCOREBOARD

The scoreboard module appears at the end of the program or after a student has chosen to leave or "exit" the program. The scoreboard can display the number of right and/or wrong responses, the percentage, and feedback regarding the total items correct. If desired, the scoreboard can appear periodically throughout the program to provide the student with a full update on their performance.

MODULE 16: PRESCRIPTION

The prescription module tells students what they should do next. It should relate to the individual student's performance and should be prescriptive in nature.

MODULE 17: END OF PROGRAM

This is the part where the student is officially thanked for working on the program. It would be appropriate to include graphics or animation to end the program. Each of these modules will be described in further detail on the following pages.

MODULE 1: IDENTIFICATION DATA

The purpose of the *identification* module is to identify important information such as the title, author, programmer, CAI type, subject, skill, date, computer system, and memory requirements. This information will not affect the lesson nor will it appear on the screen when the program is executed. Include in this section any other information that may help future users.

TITLE

The title of the program should match the one that appears on the screen. An interesting and descriptive title is recommended because your program will be one of hundreds, perhaps thousands, that are listed in catalogs. The title should indicate what the program is about without having to read the catalog description.

PROGRAM DESIGNER (AUTHOR)

Your name, as the person who designed this program, should appear next. If a different person codes the program, his or her name should follow.

PROGRAM CODER

This is the name of the person who actually wrote the program code. That way, you can each get credit for your part in creating the program.

CAI TYPE

Specify whether the program is a tutorial, review/reinforcement, or drill-and-practice type of CAI program.

SUBJECT AREA

Identify the academic subject area that your program is to be used with. This may or may not be clear from the title of your program. Even if it is self-explanatory from the title, the content area of the program should still be identified.

SKILL OR TOPIC

Most teachers like to know specifically what skill a program covers. Generally, the skill or topic is easy to identify. If it can't be identified, then you need to go back and decide what specific topic or skill your program is written for and note it here.

DATE

It is always a good idea to record the date on which a program is completed in the event that updated versions are made. Then it is easy to determine how recently a program was written or updated, or which version is being used.

COMPUTER SYSTEM

It is not always obvious from a printed copy of a program which computer system or machine a particular program is to be used on. By specifying this information in the identification data section, there is no question regarding this important piece of information.

MEMORY REQUIREMENTS

It is best to specify the minimum memory requirements in the event that an individual may have an older model of a particular computer system and may not have enough memory to use your program.

MODULE 2: TITLE

The *title* module is the first "screenful" of information to appear when the program is executed or "run." The program title, author, and copyright information should be included in this module.

The title module is where you can really use your creativity and imagination. The title is the first opportunity you have to arouse and sustain the user's interest. A catchy title is important because you want to grab his or her attention immediately. Color, graphics, and/or animation would definitely enhance this module. It is advisable, however, to use moderation when constructing this section. You want the learner to continue with the program, and if the title module is too exciting, there is a possibility that students will spend their time running the title only and never proceed with the rest of the program.

TITLE

The program title should match the title listed in the identification module. Since this is the users' first exposure to the program, the title should be as attractive as possible. A title displayed in color or graphically presented is a good way to entice the user to continue with the program.

AUTHOR(s) AND COPYRIGHT

Your name and the copyright date should appear somewhere on the screen. Color is not necessary unless this information is woven into a graphic design.

MODULE 3: NAMING/PURPOSE

The *naming/purpose* module personalizes the program because it asks the users their names. The user's name will appear throughout the program and allows the student to interact with the computer on a more personal basis.

After the computer has asked the learner's name, the *purpose* of the program should then be explained. This gives the student a *mind set* and prepares the learner for the activity in the program. In the mastery learning model, this part would be called the "anticipatory set."

When explaining the purpose of the program, it is best to keep the explanation as short as possible, yet you should give learners enough information so that they will know what they are doing. For example, you may wish to use one of the following formats:

"Today you are going to be learning about _____ because it relates to _____."

(or)

"You are going to be working on _____ because _____."

It is wise to tell the student the *reason* for working on a particular program. Oftentimes, the concept may relate to a skill that the student has acquired previously. These previously acquired skills are called "cognitive entry skills." If the students can associate the present concept to a past, similar learning, they will be able to master the current skill more quickly and easily, and the chances for success are maximized.

MODULE 4: PRETEST

The pretest is an excellent assessment tool and has several purposes. First, it can be used diagnostically to assess a student's ability level—beginning, intermediate, or advanced. Using the results from the pretest, the computer will then branch to an appropriate level in the program. In addition, the pretest simply can be used to measure how much a student knows. It is always helpful to know exactly what skills the learners have already mastered before they begin to work through a program.

If a student achieves mastery level on the pretest, then there is no need for the learner to work through the program. It would then be more appropriate for the student to proceed to another section in the menu.

When constructing the pretest, it is recommended that the posttest be constructed at the same time. This will ensure the reliability and coordination of both instruments. Your questions should be constructed to *measure a student's competency level according to the predetermined objectives*. It is very important to match each question to your objectives so that you are accurately measuring the student's knowledge of the content to be presented.

After the skill level has been determined, the student will work through the appropriate program. The posttest will then determine if the objectives have been achieved and the content fully mastered.

MODULE 5: MENU

The *menu module* can be compared to a table of contents. The menu lists the topics or skill areas on the program. It is important to provide directions on how to make a selection from the menu.

The menu itself should be divided into specific skills or topics that all relate to the overall objectives. The task analysis is useful when constructing the menu. Each section of the menu could be taken directly from the task analysis benchmarks. Mastery of each section of the menu would be required to master the entire concept being presented.

For example, if your program is designed to instruct a student in solving mathematical word problems, your menu may look like this:

MATHEMATICS WORD PROBLEMS

(A) What are they asking you?
(B) Identification of key words.
(C) Identifying the operation needed.
(D) Solving the whole word problem.
(E) Exit the program.

Similarly, afer choosing a specific item from the menu, the program may branch to another screen that will ask the learner the level of difficulty desired: easy, average, or hard.

Other menu samples may look as follows:

PARTS OF SPEECH

(A) Nouns
(B) Verbs
(C) Adjectives
(D) Adverbs
(E) Identifying them all
(F) Exit the program

It is essential to plan your menu carefully because you are actually constructing several small programs within one main subject area. Again, use your task analysis of skills to construct your lesson for each section of the menu.

Menus may provide a choice of levels of difficulty:

WHICH LEVEL DO YOU WANT TO WORK ON?

(1) Beginning   (1) Easy
(2) Medium   (2) Average
(3) Advanced   or   (3) Difficult
(4) Exit the Program   (4) Exit the Program

Another way to designate difficulty levels is by ordering the items from easy to difficult according to:

WHICH PROBLEMS DO YOU WANT TO START WITH?

(A) Problems 1-10
(B) Problems 11-20

(C) Problems 21-30
(D) Problems 31-40
(E) Problems 41-50
(F) Exit the program

The menu module should include an "exit the program" option because it allows the student to exit the program if desired. After the choice has been made, the computer will then branch back to the main menu so the student can go to another part of the program or exit the program altogether.

MODULE 6: DIRECTIONS

The *directions* module is one of the most important parts of the program because it tells the user (1) *what* to do and (2) *how* to do it. Directions may appear in several places in the courseware, depending on where it is needed. For example:

(1) At the *beginning* of the program;
(2) After each *menu* choice; or
(3) Whenever something *different* is to be done.

HOW TO WRITE CLEAR DIRECTIONS

Clear, easy-to-understand directions are important, but they are not easy to write. Here are some hints that may help:

1. *Brainstorm* and make a list of the steps in the directions. Reorder them in the correct sequence. Eliminate unnecessary steps. Rewrite items that are not clear.

2. Write the directions as if primary grade students will be using them. Write the directions *below* your students' reading levels.

3. Keep the instructions *brief*—no more than ten words per sentence. Double space between lines of text to make the directions easier to read.

4. *Show and tell* the user (a) *what* to do and (b) *how* to do it. Use illustrations, diagrams, or demonstrations. Assume nothing!

5. *Field-test* your directions on at least three students.

6. Observe the adage, KISS: Keep It Short and Simple.

MENU CHOICE

After the user has made a menu choice, restate what the person's choice was, followed by directions on *what* to do and *how* to do it.

DEMONSTRATE OR MODEL THE BEHAVIOR

Model the expected behavior so the learner knows what to do and how to do it. The directions should include a *practice item* that simulates the actual items that are to be practiced. This way, if the user has any problems, hopefully it will be with the *content* and not with how to *use* the computer or the program.

It is important that the user know whether they are to use the *return key* or whether they are to press the *space bar.* Routine behavior should not get in the way of learning—and modeling the expected behavior through a sample item will minimize this problem. Otherwise, confusion can hinder how well students perform on tasks that have a time limit.

LET THE USER CONTROL THE RATE OF READING

Students read at different rates and allowances should be made for this. Learners can control the rate of reading by using programs designed to let them decide when to go on to the next frame by pressing the space bar.

The technique of *"press the space bar to continue"* is good because the user can decide *when* to press the space bar. It should be pointed out that the space bar is recommended over the use of the return key because the learners do not have to take their eyes off the screen to look for the return key. Taking the eyes off the screen can momentarily interrupt the train of thought. The space bar can be easily accessed anywhere along the bottom of the keyboard with the thumb, whereas the return key may be inadvertantly confused with the *shift key, control key,* or *arrow keys* if the user does not stop to look or if they are using a new computer with an unfamiliar keyboard.

SKIPPING DIRECTIONS

Students who are familiar with the format of a program that is part of a courseware series or who have previously used a particular program do not need directions. If this is the case, provide the option of skipping the directions.

ASKING FOR ASSISTANCE IN THE MIDDLE OF THE PROGRAM

Provisions should be made for students to ask for help or directions while they are in the middle of the program, without having to start the program all over again from the beginning.

USER PROOF PROGRAMS

Students who get stuck in the middle of a program or who have problems booting up the program should not have to interrupt the teacher. Instead, they should be able to break out of the program and/or be able to restart the program quickly and easily.

MODULE 7: LESSON/CONTENT

The *lesson* or *content* module is the most important part of the program. This section contains either:

(1)   The lesson to be taught,
(2)   The items to be practiced, or
(3)   The test to be administered,

depending on the CAI function. This is the time when your teaching talents and creativity come into play!

When creating an educational program, it is imperative to determine the CAI technique well before the designing process begins because the structure of the lesson varies slightly depending on the technique chosen. The following is a set of guidelines for construction of drill-and-practice, tutorial, and testing lessons.

DRILL-AND-PRACTICE

In a drill-and-practice program, it is important to determine the educational objective. The questions should be structured to match the objective and to give the learner as much practice as possible to achieve mastery. It is imperative to look at the task analysis of skills prepared earlier and to focus on one objective at a time. Obviously, if there is only one objective, the practice will be comparatively short. However, if there are multiple objectives of increasing difficulty, the practice will be more comprehensive.

In a drill-and-practice program, it may be desirable to include a mini-tutorial if a student is experiencing difficulty. For example, if a student gets three in a row incorrect, it may be wise to give the learner a brief refresher course to reteach or review the basic concept. The student can then redo the questions or simply continue with the program. The mini-tutorial should be a screenful of information or graphic representation. Questions are not necessary as they will be given an opportunity to demonstrate their skill when they return to the program.

It may be appropriate to include a mini-tutorial at the beginning of a drill-and-practice program. This will review the concept prior to the actual practice and insure a higher rate of success.

TUTORIAL

The tutorial program is a bit more complicated than a simple drill-and-practice. The tutorial is an actual lesson that teaches a specific skill or concept in a predetermined content area. This type of program is best used as a supplementary or alternative teaching method. It is also useful to use with a student who has been absent and who needs to "catch up" with the rest of the class. It is important to remember, however, that the teacher should always be viewed as the primary source of instruction.

It is imperative to coordinate each screenful of information to be learned with the task analysis of skills. The screen should teach to only one objective and the questions on the screen should relate to the objective. At this point, you are simply matching your lesson to each objective in the task analysis. (See screen for specific example.)

TESTING

A testing program is not an actual lesson. However, the test may be constructed according to the task analysis previously constructed. Three to five questions are usually sufficient to measure mastery of each skill in the task analysis. For example, if your task analysis has 12 objectives, the testing program may consist of 36 questions. Again, what you are doing is simply matching test items to the skills listed in the task analysis.

COMPUTER ENRICHED INSTRUCTION

Simulation, modeling, and problem solving are all designed to extend and enhance learning. These types of programs are more complex and are not within the scope of this book.

MODULE 8: MINI-TUTORIAL

The *mini-tutorial* is an excellent teaching device in drill-and-practice programs. It can be used at the beginning of the practice to review the concept being presented, or, if a student misses several items in a row, the mini-tutorial could appear immediately to review the concept. It is wise to have a separate mini-tutorial for each skill in the menu to minimize confusion. If a pretest is included in a drill-and-practice program, a mini-tutorial may also be appropriate. Based on those questions missed, students would automatically move to the appropriate mini-tutorial for a refresher, and then proceed with the main program. This is a time-saving device as students will not have to work through an entire drill-and-practice. Rather, they will focus on just those items or skills where practice is needed.

MODULE 9: FEEDBACK

Comments to correct and incorrect responses give the learners information about how they are doing in the lesson. *Feedback* comments may be interwoven throughout the program or placed in a subroutine at the end of the program.

Record keeping may be a part of this module so that every time a student gets an answer correct, the computer is programmed to keep track of the right and wrong answers.

It is important to use sound educational psychology when providing feedback to students. Responses to both correct and incorrect answers should be sincere, realistic, and helpful. Comments should guide the student toward the correct response through a technique called "coaching." Coaching will be dealt with in the next section.

RESPONSES TO CORRECT ANSWERS

Creative feedback may be generated by brainstorming a list of possible responses. Some of the more *common* types of positive feedback comments include:

Excellent.	*You're so brilliant.*	*What a whiz you are!*
Correct.	*You're so smart.*	*You're a superstar!*
Great.	*What a brain you are!*	*You're a genius.*
Super.	*You're on a roll now.*	*Perfect.*
Terrific.	*Top notch!*	*Good work.*
Wonderful.	*Fine and dandy.*	*Terrific.*
That's correct.	*Right! Pat yourself on the back.*	
That's right.	*A-Ok!*	
That's great.	*You're thinking!*	

In creating quizzes of their own, students often make up responses based on a *theme*. One fifth-grade student based her comments on the Looney Tunes cartoon characters:

You're the pick of the carrot patch, Lisa. You got it right!

You got it R-R-R-Right!!!

The Road Runner says, "Beep-Beep! You got it right!"

Muy bien, amigo!

"You're perfectly wight," says Elmer Fudd.

You did, you did, you got it right!

You have finished the Looney Tunes Math Quiz and you have succeeded. Good work!

Other students have used their creativity in making their positive responses *rhyme,* such as these:

Good show. You're a pro!

Out of sight—that's so right!

That's a snap. This wasn't a trap!

Wow! You got it now!!!

RESPONSES TO INCORRECT ANSWERS

Some of the more conventional responses to incorrect student answers include:

Please try again.

Think that one over.

Sorry, Donna. That's not correct.

Sorry, Christine. That's not right.

One more time, please!

Put your thinking cap on.

That was close. Look again.

Whoops!

Oh! Oh! You made a boo-boo!

Too bad. Choose another answer.

Don't give up.

Don't quit.

Sorry, but that's not right.

Better try that one again, Camille.

Think about that again.

Good try, but it's not quite right.

Nope! Try again.

Examples of the Looney Tunes theme-related responses to incorrect answers include:

Bugs Bunny says no carrots. You got it wrong, so try it again, Debra!

Daffy Duck says that's despicable, Doreen. Do it over.

Porky Pig says "Th-th-that's wrong, Derek. D-d-d-do it over!"

"Beep-beep," says the Road Runner. Try it over again, Erika. Beep-beep!

Speedy Gonzales says "Wrong amigo. Do it otra vez!"

Elmer Fudd says "You cwazy wabbit. Do it over again."

Tweety Bird says I think you got it wrong . Do it over."

Sylvester says "Suffering succatosh! You blew it, Jessica! Give it another try!"

Wile E. Coyote, genius and inventor, says, "If at first you don't succeed—then try, try again!"

Rhyming examples include:

Ding-dong, you got it wrong!

Put your brain on a train!

It's sad, but that's bad.

It's a pain, but you'll have to do it over again!

Nope, you dope!

It's wrong. So long.

Good night—that's not right!

Egad! That's pretty bad!

MODULE 10: COACHING

The saying that "every champ needs a coach" is especially true of learners who are going to be successful students. Thus, the concept of *coaching* is that of providing feedback to give learners information that will assist them in getting the correct answer.

WRONG ANSWERS SHOULD BE A TEACHING TOOL

Wrong answers can be used as a *teaching tool* through the process of coaching. There are coaching techniques for answers that are *anticipated* and for those that are *unanticipated*. *Anticipated incorrect answers* are those that one could reasonably expect students to get wrong, such as the foils in a multiple choice format. *Unanticipated incorrect answers* are more like to occur in open-ended questions where students compose their own answers than when students select from among given choices such as in multiple choice or matching items. Unanticipated answers are often difficult to predict and are therefore more difficult to provide coaching that will help the learner use the incorrect material to arrive at the correct one.

ANTICIPATED ANSWERS

A well-constructed item is one in which each of the possible choices, or foils, is a *reasonable possible answer.* Anticipated answers work well with multiple choice questions. In the example below, each of the answers may be "correct" depending on how the student calculated the problem. When a wrong choice is made, the computer can be programmed to "coach" or remind the student that the order of operations is not necessarily from left to right, but that it must follow the order of operations (multiplication or division—whichever appears first from left to right—then addition followed by subtraction).

ITEM: What is the answer to: $1 + 2 - 3 * 4 / 5$
a. 0
b. 1/2
c. 1/4

Open-ended formats sometimes make it difficult to provide specific feedback. The computer can be programmed to "search" for key letters or key words. With word Mississippi, for example, a student could misspell it and still get partial or full credit because all of the letters (or characters) exist in the student's answer. The programmer could instruct the computer to "read" a string that contains certain letters and then count it as correct if it has most or all of the letters regardless of order. When a word is spelled incorrectly, full or partial credit may be given. Then the computer could display the message "Yes, that's the right answer, but it is not spelled correctly. It should be spelled *Mississippi.*"

UNANTICIPATED RESPONSES

"Off-the-wall" answers fall into the category of unanticipated responses. It is difficult for the computer to make a qualitative evaluation since computers are not able to make judgements. If the answer is totally off the wall, the computer can guide the user back into the correct channel of thinking by providing clues.

Be sure to *field test* your program and watch for answers that students may use that you may not have thought about. If unanticipated answers occur frequently, it may be that the question or item may not be well constructed. Teachers have been known to ask "false questions" when a majority of students respond with "incorrect" answers (that is, answers the teacher was not looking for). Be sure that your items are not misleading ones. It is important to field test your courseware because students will do things that you may not have thought of! At the present time, few courseware programs include coaching, but it is important that students should have an opportunity to *learn from their mistakes.*

MODULE 11: RECORD KEEPING

The *record keeping* module keeps track of all correct and incorrect responses in the program. When the student has completed the program, the total is then reported at the end of the program in the *scoreboard* module. Students may be kept informed about their progress (1) on an ongoing basis, (2) at the end of the each section, or (3) at the end of the entire program.

RIGHT AND WRONG ANSWERS

Each item should be coded so the computer can keep track of the number of total right and wrong answers. Every time the student gets an answer right or wrong, the computer can be programmed to add one more to the total correct or incorrect.

SCOREBOARD

The *scoreboard* is a summary of right and wrong answers that is displayed at the end of the program. If a student got all of the items correct, the computer could be programmed to suggest to the student what to do next. (For example, "Since you got all of the items correct, you may go on to the next unit because you have shown a thorough understanding of computer literacy.")

The difference between the record keeping and scoreboard modules is that recored keeping is an ongoing part of the program after each item. It is usually imbedded within each response line—where you respond with "That's correct!" or "Sorry, that's wrong."

The scoreboard reports the totals at the end, similar to a scoreboard at a sports event—it gives the total (points). The program's scoreboard module displays a total of all the items that were right and wrong, and sometimes even a percentage.

The computer may also be coded so that it provides comments based on the total number of items correct. For example, when a student gets more than 8 correct, the computer could make a comment such as "Keep up the fine work!" If a student gets less than 5 items correct, the computer could say "You need more practice on this skill. Please go to your textbook and reread pp. 45-60. If you have any questions, please see your teacher before you use this program again."

ITEM ANALYSIS

Ideally, the items are also coded by skill or content. That way, a summary of the types of items missed provides the teacher with information for planning future lessons, making assignments and homework, or providing information for the purpose of diagnosis and remediation.

FORMULAS

The formulas for keeping track of right and wrong items are: $R = R + 1$ (for right responses) or $W = W + 1$ (for wrong responses.) When coding items by skill or content, simply use the first letter of the skill or content. For example, in prefixes, suffixes, and root words, the formulas could be: $P = P + 1$ (for prefixes), $S = S + 1$ (for suffixes), and $RW = RW + 1$ (for root words). Please notice that you may use two letters in the code.

MODULE 12: POSTTEST

The *posttest* is an evaluative device that is used to measure a student's mastery level of the concepts in the lesson. It should be composed of questions that measure mastery of the identified major learnings or benchmarks. Ideally, the posttest should be constructed at the same time that the pretest is made. By constructing the instruments simultaneously, reliability of the instruments is enhanced.

In a drill-and-practice program, the posttest allows the instructor to monitor a student's progress. Based on the results of the test, the teacher can make the appropriate prescription for the student: The student may need to (1) redo the drill-and-practice program, (2) work on another program that allows practice of the same skill, (3) proceed to a more difficult level, or (4) simply move on to a new skill.

In a tutorial, a posttest is mandatory. It is the only way the instructor can determine if the learner has indeed worked through the entire program and has mastered the skills presented. The posttest items in a tutorial program should be constructed according to the benchmarks in the task analysis. Each question should be coordinated with the coded benchmarks concepts or skills. Again, the results of the test can be used as a basis for prescription so that the instructor can make meaningful educational decisions for the learner.

MODULE 13: EXIT

The *exit* module enables the user to exit or get out of the program at predetermined points. Some of the options are:

(1) After each item,
(2) After getting three successive items correct on the first try,
(3) After a benchmark, milestone, or criterion item, or
(4) After the completion of one section of a program.

RECOGNITION OF STUDENT DIFFERENCES

It is silly to require capable students to complete every item on a program if they have demonstrated mastery of a concept after getting four or five practice items correct.

After Each Item.　The exit option may be available upon the completion of each item in the lesson or content module. For good students, this is not a problem. But for less capable students whom we may want to complete at least a block of practice items or an entire section, the exit option after each item should not be provided.

After Three to Five Successive Correct Responses.　When students have gotten three to five items correct, it is an indication that they have mastered the concept. Because it may be boring to work through another half dozen problems, perhaps the option to exit may be available. In some courseware, the program may branch to a higher level of difficulty rather than letting the student exit the program.

Benchmarks.　One way to draw a midway line between requiring all students to complete all items, or not allowing lower ability students an option to get out of a program, is to use benchmark or milestone items. Benchmark items are keyed into the instructional objectives and are usually at the synthesis level of thinking. If students are capable enough to get a benchmark item correct, then they deserve the option of exiting that part of the program and going onto something else.

After Each Section.　The option to exit the program may be provided at the end of each section. Depending on the program, a section may be upwards of ten items so students cannot quit the program until they have completed at least that many practice items.

AN IMPORTANT FEATURE FOR PREVIEWERS

Demonstration disks and programs that educators preview should definitely contain an exit module. An experienced reviewer can size up a program in five minutes and does not need to be bored with going through an entire program to find out what it's like. Many teachers have noted that few courseware programs have an exit option, as part of the main menu or integrated throughout the program. Instead, they are forced to turn off the computer in order to get out of the program!

Although the exit module is a nice feature for those who preview programs, it may not be such a good feature for students—especially young students or lower ability students. For these users, the exit module may give them a choice we may not want them to have!

SUMMARY

Exit is one of the selections on the main menu. When a student decides to exit from a particular part of the program, they should first be taken back to the main menu so they can either make another selection or exit. If, at that point, the student really wants to stop workng on that program, then the exit section can be made.

Once the exit module is selected, the scoreboard, assignment (prescription), closure, and end of program follow.

MODULE 14: CLOSURE/REVIEW

Every lesson must have a *closure* or *review* module. Too often, teachers leave students "hanging" at the end of a lesson; and educational computer software often leaves the user without the benefit of closure as well. Closure or review enhances the possibility of retaining the concept for a longer period of time. Just as the naming/ purpose module establishes a "mind set" and prepares the user for what they will be learning, the closure/review module "ends" the lesson and establishes a definite termination point for the concept being presented.

When writing a closure/review module, begin by personalizing your comment and then tell the student exactly what they have just learned. It is important to be specific so that the learning will be crystalized for the student. If several major concepts have been presented, it is essential to review the major highlights of each concept. The review/closure module should not be long. Its function is to review the concepts taught and to provide a definite ending point to the lesson.

MODULE 15: SCOREBOARD

The *scoreboard* module appears at the end of the program and displays the total correct responses and the total incorrect responses. It may appear (1) at the end of the program, (2) at the time students choose to exit the program, (3) after student have completed all of the items in the program, (4) whenever students wish to see how they are doing, or, (5) periodically, to give students an ongoing progress report. The scoreboard module may display one or more of the following:

- Total right and total wrong
- Percentage of items right and wrong
- Feedback on total items correct

APPROPRIATE COMMENTS IMPORTANT

Scoreboard comments may be provided throughout the program. If a student gets all of the items correct, the computer could be programmed to display the following messages on the screen. These comments assess the level of success. For example:

YOU SCORED 10 OUT OF 10 CORRECT. YOU DID AN EXCELLENT JOB AND SHOWED THAT YOU REALLY LEARNED HOW TO _____. YOU REALLY KNOW YOUR STUFF!

YOU SCORED 9 OUT OF 10 CORRECT. THAT'S TERRIFIC WORK!

YOU SCORED 8 OUT OF 10 CORRECT. THAT'S VERY GOOD WORK.

PRESCRIPTIVE/COMMENTS

If students fared poorly, provide a prescriptive comment based on an item analysis of the types of items missed.

YOU SCORED 6 OUT OF 10 CORRECT. GO BACK AND REREAD PAGES 123-130 IN "NEW FRONTIERS."

YOU SCORED 3 OUT OF 10 CORRECT. YOU SHOULD SEE YOUR TEACHER ABOUT . . .

FORMULAS

If you want the computer to print out the total of the correct answers, use

? R "Correct Answers"

If you want the computer to print out the total of the incorrect answers, use

? W "Incorrect Answers"

If you want the computer to display a percentage of the total correct, then use the formula

R = Right Answers

T = Total Items

? R / T

MODULE 16: PRESCRIPTION/ASSIGNMENT

The *prescription* or assignment module is an essential element of any educational program. It enables the teacher to relate and integrate the learning via the computer to the existing curriculum in the classroom. Unfortunately, computers are often used in isolation and fail to relate to the current course of study in the classroom. The prescription module prevents this from happening.

This module can restate the number of correct responses for the student. Based on this number, the student should be directed toward appropriate prescriptive activities that will review, reinforce, or extend the learning. For example, a student may need to redo the program, proceed to a different program to practice the same skill, or go on to a more difficult skill or concept. The learner could also be directed to see the teacher, to read specific pages in a text that relates to the program, or to read new textbook material in preparation for a future computer lesson. Whatever the assignment, it should be prescriptive in nature and based on the results of the student's achievement.

MODULE 17: END OF PROGRAM

The end of the entire program should have a screen thanking the student for their participation. This lets the student know that they are completely finished with the lesson. Just as the purpose module prepares the student for the learning and gives the learner a "mind set" for the activity to follow, the *end of program* screen closes the learning for the student and gives the learner a sense of completeness.

It is a good idea to personalize your statements and to include color, graphics, and/or sound. There are many ending remarks that can be used, such as "Over and out!" "That's all folks!" or just simply, "The End." Here is a chance for you to be imaginative and create your own final words!

4 Sample Lesson

- Title Module
- Naming/Purpose Module
- Menu
- Directions
- Sample Pretest
- Sample Lesson
- Sample Questions for Lessons
- Mini-Tutorials
- Sample Posttest
- Sample Screens

This chapter contains a sample lesson that illustrates the principles outlined in the modules described in Chapter 3. This will give you a concrete idea of how the theory is put into practice.

TITLE MODULE

THE WORLD OF COMPUTERS

By

Julie Chan and Marilyn Korostoff

NAMING/PURPOSE MODULE

**Welcome to
the World of Computers**

What is your name?

(Name), you are going to learn about several different topics in the field of computers. It is important because in the current computer age, one must know as much about the different aspects of computers as possible.

—Press the space bar to continue—

MENU

Where would you like to begin?

Type in the number of your choice and press the RETURN key.

- (1) Computer Careers
- (2) Computer Applications
- (3) Computers and the Future
- (4) Exit the program

DIRECTIONS

Directions

1. You chose to work on Computer Applications.
   (Good choice!)

2. Information about computer applications will appear on the screen. Read the information carefully.

3. Periodically throughout the program, several questions will appear that relate to the material you have just read.

4. Answer each question by typing in the letter of your answer. Press the return key after answering each question.
   Have a good time!

—Press the space bar to continue—

SAMPLE PRETEST

Each question of the pretest should be coordinated with each objective in the task analysis.

PRETEST

Here is a pretest to see just what you already know about computer applications. Answer each question by typing in the letter of your answer.

1. Computers can be used for

    a. police records
    b. making decisions
    c. both
    d. none of the above

2. A major computer application area is

    a. information storage
    b. information retrieval
    c. both
    d. none of the above

    —Press the space bar to continue—

3. Computers can be used for

    a. teaching
    b. video games
    c. both
    d. none of the above

4. A major computer application area is

    a. giving personal advice
    b. simulations
    c. both
    d. none of the above

    —Press the space bar to continue—

5. Computers can be used for

    a. robotics
    b. transportation systems
    c. both
    d. none of the above

6. A major computer application area is

    a. rocketry
    b. process control
    c. both
    d. none of the above

    —Press the space bar to continue—

7. Computers can be used for

    a.   chossing a job
    b.   preparing meals
    c.   both
    d.   none of the above

8. A major computer application area is

    a.   computation
    b.   weather forecasting
    c.   both
    d.   none of the above

—Press the space bar to continue—

9. Computers can be used for

    a.   banking
    b.   billing
    c.   both
    d.   none of the above

10. A major computer application area is

    a.   financial management
    b.   data processing
    c.   both
    d.   none of the above

—Press the space bar to continue—

11. Computers can be used for

    a.   typing
    b.   writing books
    c.   both
    d.   none of the above

12. A major computer application area is

    a.   word processing
    b.   preparing reports
    c.   both
    d.   none of the above

—Press the space bar to continue—

SAMPLE LESSON

The following is a sample lesson to be coordinated with objective 1 from the task analysis.

Objective 1: Students will recognize the appropriate information storage and retrieval functions of the computer.

COMPUTER APPLICATIONS

Lesson 1

Computers have many uses and can be applied in various areas. For example, computers are now being used to manage personal checkbooks. The user simply types in the purpose and the amount of the check. The computer immediately lists the balance in the checking account. The computer can be programmed to identify checks that are tax deductible and at the end of the year the user can simply request that the computer retrieve this pertinent tax information. The computer can also be programmed to identify specific areas where checks have been used; that is, food, entertainment, school expenses, clothes, and so on.

As you can see, using a computer as a checkbook manager can save a lot of time.

—Press the space bar to continue—

Lesson 1 continued

Students can also use computers to create their own programs. After learning some basic programming skills, students can design programs to help them learn almost any skill or they can even create their own adventure games. As students complete portions of their programs, the information can easily be saved on a disk or cassette tape. The next time a student wants to work on the program, they will simply retrieve the information from the disk or cassette, load it into the computer's memory, and begin where they left off.

It's always nice not to have to start all over again from the beginning.

—Press the space bar to continue—

Lesson 1 continued

Computers are used to store mailing lists. When businesses need to advertise to their customers, the computer retrieves the stored names and addresses of prospective buyers and prints labels. The business can attach the labels to envelopes and the advertisement is sent out. Without the computer, it would be necessary to handwrite all addresses. Needless to say, the computer saves an enormous amount of time.

—Press the space bar to continue—

Lesson 1 continued

The Internal Revenue Service uses computers extensively. Due to the enormous population in the United States, all tax records on individual citizens are placed in the computer's memory. The IRS can keep track of those who pay taxes, those who don't, and determine who to audit in any tax year. Computers have clearly made the job of the IRS much easier.

—Press the space bar to continue—

Lesson 1 continued

Police agencies also use computers. An enormous amount of information regarding specific crimes, criminals, misdeameanors, felonies, and all police related information can be

> stored in the computer's memory. It is often necessary to retrieve information quickly and the computer facilitates this task.
>
> —Press the space bar to continue—

The following is a sample of the lesson to be presented after all five areas of Information Storage and Retrieval have been covered. It is coordinated with objective 2.

Objective 2: Students will indicate that computers can be used as an information storage and retrieval device.

Lesson 2

Checkbook management, creating student programs, mailing lists, IRS records, and police records are all examples of how computers are used as Information Storage and Retrieval devices. Computers are invaluable in this area. You can program a computer to store in its memory just about any piece of information. Similarly, the computer will quickly retrieve the information from its memory whenever you want.

Using the Computer as an Information Storage and Retrieval device eliminates the use of many paper files that can take up a lot of unnecessary space. Also, the computer's speed when recalling information saves a lot of valuable time.

—Press the space bar to continue—

The following is a sample of the lesson to be matched with objective 3.

Objective 3: Students will recognize the appropriate simulation functions of the computer.

Lesson 3

Computers are a great source of entertainment. Many programs ask the user to become a completely different individual, such as a fur trapper, space voyager, or pioneer. Hours and hours can be spent being entertained by the computer.

Video games are a very popular computer application. The decisions, choices, or moves made by the user can affect the outcome of the game. Video games can be found in popular arcades, however, there are many game programs that can be purchased for home use as well.

—Press the space bar to continue—

Lesson 3 continued

Computers are used extensively in the field of education. Concepts in such areas as science, math, and social science are easily taught using the computer. Students who have been absent can also use the computer to catch up on concepts they have missed. Graphic displays are an excellent and effective method of demonstrating a concept.

Airline and space flight training is another area where computers are used on a wide-scale basis. Pilots are tested as if they were in real situations and their reactions are closely monitored. They are confronted with every possible situation in order to give them adequate practice before actually flying an air or spacecraft. Pilots can learn how to fly, control, and navigate an aircraft without ever leaving the ground.

—Press the space bar to continue—

The following is a lesson to be matched with objective 4.

Objective 4: Students will indicate that computers are used as simulation devices.

Lesson 4

Entertainment, video games, teaching, and flight training are just a few examples of how computers are used as *Simulation* devices. Simulations are a great way to use the computer. In simula-

64

tion programs, the computer is used to imitate real life situations. The users are asked to pretend that they are actually in the situation and to make choices and decisions based on the situations presented. Simulations are an excellent and practical application of computers.

—Press the space bar to continue—

The following is a sample of the lesson to be matched with objective 5.

Objective 5: Students will recognize the appropriate process control functions of the computer.

Lesson 5

Did you know that the rides at Disneyland are controlled by computer? Speed, space between cars, locking devices, and all other basic functions are carefully monitored by a master computer. It is obvious that the computer system in Disneyland is very sophisticated and complex. Nonetheless, the system enables this large amusement park to run smoothly and efficiently.

Did you also know that transportation systems such as BART or subway systems are controlled by computer? The computer controls speed and departure times, but it can also tell if a train is malfunctioning or experiencing difficulties. This information is immediately transmitted to the supervisor in charge who can take the appropriate steps to clear up the difficulty.

—Press the space bar to continue—

Lesson 5 continued

Computers are also used as robots. Robotics is a fast growing field. Many tedious jobs are now being performd by robots, which free personnel to do more complicated or sophisticated tasks. In Japan, robots even take morning exercise just like the human employees.

Finally, computers are used in the field of rocketry. The space shuttle Columbia is an excellent example where just about all space functions are controlled by several computers. NASA relies heavily on the complex capabilities of computers.

As you can see, computers are used in many different areas to control different operations.

—Press the space bar to continue—

The following lesson is to be matched with objective 6.

Objective 6: Students will indicate that computers are used as process control devices.

Lesson 6

Disneyland rides, transportation systems, robotics, and rocketry are all examples of how computers are used in the area of *Process Control*. Computers are used to monitor and control mechanical operations or processes. This type of process control requires a large sophisticated system. It must be carefully monitored to ensure that all systems function smoothly and consistently.

—Press the space bar to continue—

The following lesson is matched with objective 7. Note that two specific applications, math calculation and math homework, have been combined in one paragraph.

Objective 7: Students will recognize the appropriate computation functions of the computer.

Lesson 7

The computer can be used as a calculator. It can make simple calculations or, with a more sophisticated program, the computer can perform complex functions. Many small businesses find that using the computer as a calculator can save a lot of valuable work time.

Math calculation is a specific computer application. Students find it useful to check math homework or make appropriate math computations and calculations using the computer. There are innumerable mathematical calculations that a computer can perform both accurately and quickly.

Computers can be utilized for projecting future sales. Using a specific program, businesses can project sales by entering in past sales information. The computer then analyzes the information and makes appropriate predictions. Businesses rely heavily on these predictions and make future plans based on the computer's information.

—Press the space bar to continue—

The following lesson is matched with objective 8.

Objective 8: Students will indicate that computers are used as devices for computation.

Lesson 8

The computer can be used as a calculator, for math calculations, for math homework, and to make sales projections. These are just a few examples of how computers can be used as *Computational Devices*. The computer is quite accurate and efficient in performing these functions. Using the computer for computations is a sure time-saver.

—Press the space bar to continue—

The following matches objective 9.

Objective 9: Students will recognize the appropriate data processing functions of the computer.

Lesson 9

Banks rely heavily on computers. Deposits, withdrawals, and transfers of money are just a few of the many functions the computer can perform. In addition, one's balance in a savings or checking account is accurately recorded and can be quickly retrieved. Automated tellers are completely controlled by computer. Banking can now be done on a 24-hour basis. Soon, many people will be doing their banking from their homes because home telephones will have access to the bank's computer terminal. In the future, one may never have to enter a bank again!

Many people manage finances using a computer. The financial information is analyzed and processed by the computer. Based on the computer's analysis, financial decisions and plans can be made.

—Press the space bar to continue—

Lesson 9 continued

A popular way to use the computer is as a budget manager. Many programs currently on the market regulate home budgets, organize budget records, and manage general household functions. The computer is a valuable tool in organizing a financial budget.

Computers do an excellent job managing billing processes. The computer can keep track of accounts that have been paid and those which are delinquent. The computer can be programmed to print bills on predetermined dates. Accounts are kept in an organized fashion and few billing errors can be made. The computer usually will *not* forget to send a bill!

—Press the space bar to continue—

The following lesson matches objective 10.

Objective 10: Students will indicate that computers are used as data processors.

Lesson 10

Using the computer for banking, finances, managing a budget and billing are examples of how the computer is used for *Data Processing*. Data processing can be defined as taking data or information and performing some sort of function with the data. In other words, it takes the data and does something with it. Computers can handle an enormous amount of information and process the data at an incredible speed.

—Press the space bar to continue—

The following lesson matches objective 11. Please note that all four word processing functions are combined on one screen.

Objective 11: Students will recognize the appropriate word processing functions of the computer.

Lesson 11

Computers are excellent typewriters! For example, with a word processing program, computers can be used for writing letters, research reports, books, and for preparing medical and legal reports. Information can be easily entered into the computer's memory. This information can be edited, corrected, or moved from one place to another. With another program, spelling can even be analyzed.

Using the computer to type information is an incredible time-saving device. There is no need to retype pages that have mistakes. Mistakes can be corrected individually without retyping entire passages or pages.

Obviously, using a computer as a typewriter can save an enormous amount of time.

—Press the space bar to continue—

The following lesson matches objective 12.

Objective 12: Students will indicate that computers are used as word processors.

Lesson 12

Using the computer as a typewriter for writing books, research reports, or medical and legal reports are just a few examples of how computers are used as word processors. Word Processing is simply a process of handling words. Information is entered, edited, and printed quickly and easily. The main advantage of using a computer as a word processing device is speed. Countless hours can be saved by using the computer as a word processor.

—Press the space bar to continue—

SAMPLE QUESTIONS FOR LESSONS

The following are examples of questions that can be used to assess what the students have learned in the area of computer applications. In a normal lesson, the teacher would generally include many more items than those presented. Please note that all even-numbered questions can be coded as criterion items, which test for mastery of each objective in the lesson.

SAMPLE QUESTIONS FOR LESSONS 1 AND 2

Let's see how well you read the material on Information Storage and Retrieval. Answer the following questions by typing the letter of your answer. Be sure to press the return key after each response.

1. Computers can be used for

   a. checkbook management
   b. storing student programs
   c. both
   d. none of the above

2. A major computer application area is

   a. information storage
   b. information retrieval
   c. both
   d. none of the above

SAMPLE QUESTIONS FOR LESSONS 3 AND 4

How well have you read the lesson on Simulations? Be sure to press the return key after your response.

    1. Computers can be used for

        a. teaching
        b. airline training
        c. both
        d. none of the above

    2. A major computer application area is

        a. video games
        b. simulations
        c. both
        d. none of the above

SAMPLE QUESTIONS FOR LESSONS 5 AND 6

Did you read the information on Process Control carefully? Well, let's see. Choose the letter of your response and type it in. Be sure to press the return key after typing in your answer.

    1. Computers can be used for

        a. dancing
        b. monitoring transportation systems
        c. both
        d. none of the above

    2. A major computer application area is

        a. process control
        b. monitoring mechanical functions
        c. both
        d. none of the above

SAMPLE QUESTIONS FOR LESSONS 7 AND 8

How well did you read the lesson on Computation? Don't forget to press the return key after you answer the question.

1. Computers can be used for

   a.   making calculations
   b.   adding, subtracting, multiplying and dividing
   c.   both
   d.   none of the above

2. A major computer application area is

   a.   computation
   b.   financial projections
   c.   both
   d.   none of the above

SAMPLE QUESTIONS FOR LESSONS 9 AND 10

Can you answer the following questions on Data Processing? Press the return key after you answer the question.

1. Computers can be used as

   a.   budget managers
   b.   billing devices
   c.   both
   d.   none of the above

2. A major computer application area is

   a.   data processing
   b.   data formulation
   c.   both
   d.   none of the above

SAMPLE QUESTIONS FOR LESSONS 11 and 12

Let's see how carefully you read the lesson on Word Processing. Answer the questions carefully and be sure to press the return key after your response.

1. Computers can be used for

   a.   typing
   b.   writing books

    c. both
    d. none of the above

2. A major computer application area is

    a. word processing
    b. reporting
    c. both
    d. none of the above

MINI-TUTORIALS

If a student misses three in a row, you may want the program to branch to a mini-tutorial. All of the mini-tutorials may not be used; however, it is important to provide mini-tutorials that cover all major objectives in the program.

The following mini-tutorials can be used with lessons 1 and 2, 3 and 4, 5 and 6, 7 and 8, 9 and 10, and 11 and 12, respectively.

Mini-Tutorial for Lessons 1 and 2

It seems like you need a little review on the five uses of computers in the area of Information Storage and Retrieval.

Let's review. The computer can be used (1) as a checkbook manager; (2) to save student programs; (3) to store mailing lists; (4) for IRS records; and (5) as a storage device for police records.

Now, let's go back and try again.

—Press the space bar to continue the lesson—

Mini-Tutorial for Lessons 3 and 4

Let's review the four functions of the computer in the major area of Simulations.

The computer can be used (1) for entertainment; (2) for video games; (3) for teaching; and (4) as airline and space flight training aides.

Now, let's go back and try again.

—Press the space bar to continue the lesson—

Mini-Tutorial for Lessons 5 and 6

Let's go over the uses of the computer in the area of Process Control.

The computer can be used for (1) monitoring Disneyland rides; (2) transportations systems; (3) robotics; and (4) rocketry.

Now, let's try again.

—Press the space bar to continue the lesson—

Mini-Tutorial for Lessons 7 and 8

Let's go over the functions of the computer in the major area of Computation.

Computers are used as (1) calculators; (2) math calculators; (3) math homework aids; and (4) sales projectors.

Now, let's return to the main program.

—Press the space bar to continue the lesson—

Mini-Tutorial for Lessons 9 and 10

It seems that you need to go over the computer applications in the area of Data Processing.

Computers are used (1) to perform bank functions; (2) for finance; (3) as budget managers; and (4) for billing.

Let's return to the program.

—Press the space bar to continue the lesson—

Mini-Tutorial for Lessons 11 and 12

Let's take another look at Word Processing.

The computer can be used (1) as a typewriter; (2) for writing books; (3) for research reports; and (4) for preparation of medical and legal reports.

Let's see how you do on the questions now.

—Press the space bar to continue the lesson—

SAMPLE POSTTEST

Each question of the posttest should be coordinated with each objective in the task analysis.

POSTTEST

Now let's see what you've learned.

Answer the following questions by typing in the letter of your answer. Be sure to press return after each response.

1. Computers can be used as

    a. checkbook managers
    b. for IRS records
    c. both
    d. none of the above

2. A major computer application area is

    a. information storage and retrieval
    b. evaluating books
    c. both
    d. none of the above

—Press the space bar to continue—

3. Computers can be used for

    a. entertainment
    b. buying cars
    c. both
    d. none of the above

4. A major computer application area is

    a. simulations
    b. making crafts

   c. both

   d. none of the above

—Press the space bar to continue—

5. Computers can be used for

     a.   Disneyland rides

     b.   rocketry

     c.   both

     d.   none of the above

6. A major computer application area is

     a.   typing

     b.   singing

     c.   both

     d.   none of the above

—Press the space bar to continue—

7. Computers can be used for

     a.   math calculations

     b.   sales projections

     c.   both

     d.   none of the above

8. A major computer application area is

     a.   homework

     b.   calculations

     c.   both

     d.   none of the above

—Press the space bar to continue—

9. Computers can be used for

     a.   billing

     b.   finance

     c.   both

     d.   none of the above

10. A major computer application area is

    a. budgeting
    b. data processing
    c. both
    d. none of the above

—Press the space bar to continue—

---

11. Computers can be used for

    a. typing
    b. preparing research reports
    c. both
    d. none of the above

12. A major computer application area is

    a. handling words
    b. word processing
    c. both
    d. none of the above

—Press the space bar to continue—

Congratulations, Jonathan! You have just finished the posttest on computer applications.

—Press the space bar to continue—

SAMPLE SCREENS

Sample Feedback Screen for Correct Responses

Awesome, (Name)!!!!

You're really cooking!

Way to go!

Sample Coaching Screen for Anticipated Incorrect Responses

Would you like some help, (Name)?

Do you need a clue?

Sample Coaching Screen for Unanticipated Incorrect Answers

That doesn't sound right to me.
Let's think this through again.

Sample Prescription Screen

Assignment

(Name,) you got 20 right out of 20 questions.

Now you need to get ready for your next program.

You can choose another program from the menu or you can wait until you visit the computer again to start another program.

—Press the space bar to continue—

Sample End of Program Screen

The End

We'll see you again, (name)!!!

Thanks for doing such a GREAT job on this lesson!

Over and out!

Sample Closure and Review Screen

Closure and Review

You have just completed a lesson on Computer Applications.

You learned that there are six major areas where computers are used. You also learned some specific applications in each computer area. There are many more specific computer applications, but in this lesson you learned about some of the most important ones!

—Press the space bar to continue—

Sample Scoreboard Screen

(Name), here is how you did on this lesson:

Total right: 20

Total wrong: 0

Percentage of right answers: 100%

Percentage of wrong answers: 0%

You are a super student! Congratulations!!!

—Press the space bar to continue—

5 Coding Your Courseware

- Doing It Yourself
- Getting Someone to Do It for You
- Using an Authoring Tool

Once you have designed your courseware, you will need to program or *code* it for use on the microcomputer. There are several alternatives to programming your software creation: You may elect to do it yourself, especially if you have taken a course or two in programming in any of several popular languages suitable for microcomputers; you may get someone to do it for you; or you may use an authoring tool. This section describes the features of each alternative, along with its advantages and disadvantages.

DOING IT YOURSELF

Teachers who have learned how to program in BASIC, LOGO, or PASCAL will find the challenge of designing their own classroom courseware appealing. The advantage of programming your own software is that you can work on it as diligently (or as sparingly) as you wish, include as many features (or bells and whistles) as you want, and have the freedom to write, rewrite, revise, or refine it as often as needed. You should realize, however, that you'll never be totally happy with your own "finished" product because you'll always think of ways to improve your program!

For the total novice with only a few computer programming workshops or introductory-level classes, the thought of writing a program may seem overwhelming. Unless you have a solid programming course or two under your belt, or unless you are a self-taught hacker who spends tons of time playing around with the computer (writing programs—not playing games!), you may want to consider teaming up with an experienced programmer who knows microcomputers if you still insist on doing it yourself.

You should be forewarned that programming can be a very time-consuming process. Experienced programmers use a rule of thumb that says to allow about half as much time to debug a program as to write it. In other words, for every ten minutes of programming, allow about five minutes for debugging. For a true beginner, the time spent on debugging could be much more than this!

Nonetheless, for those of you who do enjoy programming, writing your own courseware for classroom use can be a real high! Just as most of us teachers who enjoy creating materials to use with our students find it to be a rewarding experience, creating software for our students to use at the computer is just as much fun and just as fulfilling.

GETTING SOMEONE TO DO IT FOR YOU

Teaming up with an experienced programmer to get your courseware coded is an efficient way to approach the programming challenge. If you are still fairly new to computers and are a total novice at programming, working with an experienced programmer may net you a program that is ten times better and possibly completed with one-tenth the effort it might take if you were to complete it by yourself!

However, it is far better that *you* design the courseware, because as a teacher you know teaching and learning theory and you understand how students learn best in your content area. Also, teachers are curriculum specialists, so they know their course content and what students need to learn.

It is important that you work closely with whomever you choose as your the programmer. You should also have a working knowledge of computers so you will know what demands you can make of the computer and what features to tell the programmer to include in your courseware. Unless you know a little about the capabilities of computers, you may not be tapping their full potential.

As the programmer codes each major portion, you should be on hand to try it out to make sure that the program is working the way you had planned, with all of the features that you demand. It could also turn out that the programmer, if he or she is a good one, may suggest features and embellishments that you may not have considered. The most important thing is that you two work closely as a team to reach the goal of completing the courseware program.

One drawback may be the fact that this person works as a programmer and may not be thrilled with having to program during his or her off hours. Unless there is financial gain to be had, either through an attractive fee or through a percentage of the royalties or potential profits, the appeal may not be there.

Some sources for part-time programmers include students who are computer science majors at local colleges and universities, students who are taking programming classes at your own school or at a nearby high school in your district, acquaintances who enjoy programming as a hobby, or friends who are professional programmers for corporations or businesses. (Some educators I know are married to programmers, so they have a built-in team!)

Fees for programming vary, depending on the individual's experience, motivation for taking on your project (for the experience, for another "credit" in a publishing list, for the potential royalties, or whatever), and how much time he or she is willing to spend on the project. It is recommended that you offer a flat fee for the entire project rather than pay on an hourly basis, because the total hours may be a staggering number!

USING AN AUTHORING TOOL

A third alternative is that of using authoring tools, which include *authoring programs* and *authoring languages*. An authoring program lets you create computer courseware without being able to program; an authoring language is a simplified programming language, such as PILOT.

AUTHORING PROGRAMS

The advantage of an authoring program is that you can use it off the shelf, as is. After learning how to use the program, you merely answer a series of questions, which then creates the computer activity for you. However, one of the drawbacks of most authoring programs is that most allow only drill-and-practice-type activities. But if this is what you are after anyway, they are fine.

Some of the more widely used programs are (1) THE GAME SHOW (Apple Software), which is similar to a television game show such as the *Family Feud*. Contestants take turns answering questions, and the points decrease as contestants miss their turns. Teachers and students enjoy this game format to review or practice recall or knowledge-level items. (2) CREATE (Hartley) is an easy-to-use package that displays the text in large, manuscript print. This feature is advantageous for primary grade students. (3) Computerized Lesson Authoring Systems (CLAS, by Touch Technologies) enables you to create a single lesson on a single topic or an entire semester's course for the computer. CLAS presents items in either random or sequential order.

Among the more sophisticated authoring programs is Assisted Instructional Development System (AIDS, by SkillCorp). Its format is similar to the software design framework introduced in this book. The BLOCKS Authoring Program (California

School for the Deaf) contains eight disks and allows you to integrate sound, color, and animated graphics into your lesson.

AUTHORING LANGUAGES

Authoring languages such as PILOT are intended to let you create a computer lesson without your being able to program. However, learning PILOT is similar to learning BASIC or any other programming language—you still need to learn the various commands and how to use them!

One of the drawbacks to some authoring programs is that they do not include branching. Others do not have a true record-keeping system other than tallying the total number of items right and wrong: There is no provision for an item analysis from which a prescriptive assignment can be made. The programs may be as inexpensive as $30-$50, while others cost as much as $300-$500. One of the programs (AIDS) comes with a special chip to prevent copying; thus lessons created with AIDS work only on computers that also contain this special chip.

In general, authoring tools (both authoring programs and authoring languages) enable most teachers to create lessons and computer activities quickly and easily. This lets a teacher make as many computer lessons as he or she wants with a minimum of work, once the lesson content has been determined through a task analysis and the items have been written.

6 Evaluating Your Courseware

- Courseware Evaluation Guidelines
- Courseware Review Rating Form

Once you have designed your lesson and have had it programmed or coded, you will want to field-test it to be certain the bugs are corrected. Be sure to check it for spelling, punctuation, and grammatical details.

After that, use the program with your students to make sure it is "childproof."

Next, evaluate your program with one of several evaluation forms. Try to be objective in rating your program against the criteria on the form(s). You may also try asking a colleague to use your program with their students and then evaluate the program using one of the two evaluation forms that are contained in this part of the book. These forms are typical of the types of evaluation forms that school districts use to rate courseware considered for purchase and adoption by the school or district. Be sure that your courseware measures up!

COURSEWARE EVALUATION GUIDELINES

TITLE _____ SUBJECT _____

AUTHOR _____ PUBLISHER _____

PRICE _____ DISTRIBUTOR _____

COMPUTER SYSTEM _____ VERSION NO. _____

MEMORY REQUIREMENTS _____

	Outstanding Satisfactory				Poor
RATING	5	4	3	2	1	0

A. LESSON OBJECTIVES
1. The objective is clearly defined.
2. The program achieves the stated purpose.

B. CONTENT
3. The content is accurate.
4. The content is presented clearly.
5. The content is logically presented.
6. The content is free from stereotypes.

C. INSTRUCTIONAL DESIGN FEATURES
7. There is positive feedback to the learner.
8. The learning can be generalized.
9. The learner controls the rate of learning.
10. The learning is motivational.
11. The difficulty level is appropriate to the intended audience.
12. It stimulates student creativity.
13. It integrates prior learning.
14. It challenges/stimulates student thinking.
15. The lesson length is appropriate for the intended audience.
16. The record keeping system allows for instructional diagnosis.

D. PROGRAM DESIGN
17. The directions are clear.
18. The program is well written.
19. The reading level is appropriate to the intended audience.
20. The frame designs are varied.
21. The format is consistent.
22. The documentation is thorough.
23. The program can be modified by the teacher.

E. MACHINE CAPABILITIES
24. The user can operate it easily and independently.
25. The color/graphics/sound are used to best advantage.
26. The computer's capabilities are used appropriately.

F. VALIDATION
27. The program meets the stated objectives (validity).
28. The program meets use/re-use consistency (reliability).
29. The program was designed for students of similar ability or background.
30. The program was field-tested on students similar to those who are using it.

COURSEWARE REVIEW RATING FORM

1 TITLE_____

  SUBJECT _____

  GRADE LEVEL(S) _____ ABILITY LEVEL _____

  OBJECTIVE(S):

2 ____ Tutorial   ____ Simulation

  ____ Drill-&-Practice   ____ Modeling

  ____ Teacher Utility   ____ Problem Solving

  ____ Other: _____

  COMMENTS:

3 MODULES INCLUDED: (Mark a √ next to each item)

YES	NO	
____	____	Identification module
____	____	Title module
____	____	Naming module
____	____	Purpose module
____	____	Pretest module
____	____	Menu module
____	____	Directions module
____	____	Mini-Tutorial module
____	____	Lesson/Content module
____	____	Feedback module
____	____	Coaching module
____	____	Record keeping module
____	____	Exit module
____	____	Posttest module
____	____	Closure module
____	____	Scoreboard module
____	____	Prescription module
____	____	End of Program module

4 FEATURES: (Mark a √ next to each item)

YES	NO	
____	____	Color
____	____	Graphics
____	____	Animation
____	____	Sound
____	____	Voice Capabilities
____	____	Branching (Levels of Difficulty)

5 WHAT DID YOU *LIKE* ABOUT THIS PROGRAM?

6 IF THIS PROGRAM WERE TO BE REVISED, WHAT WOULD YOU CHANGE IN IT?

7 LIST WAYS THAT YOU WOULD USE THIS PROGRAM IN YOUR CLASSROOM

8 WOULD YOU RECOMMEND THIS PROGRAM FOR PURCHASE? ____ Yes ____ No ____ Maybe

  WHY?

7 Publishing, Marketing, and Selling Your Courseware

- Doing It Yourself
- Contracting with a Software Distribution Firm
- Contracting with Major Publishing Companies
- Educational Software Publishing Companies
- Resources

Once you write your educational software program and find that it works well with the students in your classes, you may begin to think about how you can share your program with other teachers who might also be able to use such a program to supplement, augment, or enhance their teaching. This next step then turns you from an author to a businessperson who markets, distributes, and sells your product.

You have several alternatives in marketing and selling your software. You can do it yourself, find a marketing firm to do it for you, or contract with a major educational or software publishing firm. Of course, there are ups and downs to each one of these options.

DOING IT YOURSELF

You may decide to market and sell your software program yourself. It is important to be aware of the advantages and drawbacks of doing it yourself.

ADVANTAGES

When you market and sell your own software, you have total control of how things are handled. You also stand to gain the most financially, once your initial costs have been recovered because all of the profits are yours alone.

DISADVANTAGES

The cost of marketing, distributing, and selling a product is estimated to be about 60% of the list price of the product itself. Once you have projected how much it will cost you to advertise, produce, handle, and ship the product, you may not be making any money for some time because any money that you make will be reinvested in the business (or to repay any loans that you may have had to make for start-up costs.) If the software is an instant success and you are still teaching full time, you may find that your weekends and evenings are spent running your fledgling educational software business. When your business grows, you may need to gain additional expertise in running a company, hire additional help, incur warehousing costs (when storing the product outgrows your apartment, the spare room in your home, or garage), and other related operating expenses. The cost of the materials such as printing and packaging also mounts up. Unless printing is done in bulk, the cost can be prohibitive—so you may have a lot of inventory laying around until you sell it.

Although there appear to be more disadvantages than advantages to running the show yourself, the pride of ownership and being an entrepreneur may outweigh the drawbacks. Many major business publications claim that "the eighties is the era of the entrepreneur." You will join those ranks should you decide to market, sell, and distribute your own educational software.

CONTRACTING WITH A SOFTWARE DISTRIBUTION FIRM

There are companies that make it their business to market and distribute products on behalf of manufacturers (you). Still, other companies do both—they will manufacture and package your software package and take it to market.

Companies such as SoftSel, Micro D, and Software Distributors distribute business, home, entertainment, and educational software to retail stores that sell hardware as well as software, and to outlets that sell software only.

Some companies such as SoftKat distribute only educational software. Mail-order companies including Scholastic, Opportunities for Learning, and Huntington handle educational software.

ADVANTAGES

The primary advantage to contracting with a distribution company is that you may sell more units because you will have a wider channel of distribution. The more available your product is, the more exposure it will get and the chances that copies will be sold are increased.

Distribution companies spend a lot of money buying display advertising space in major educational computer publications and sending out direct mail-order catalogs. In addition, they often provide press releases of new products and send review copies of your software to reviewers for publication purposes.

DISADVANTAGES

The initial product screening process is stringent because most distribution companies want to be sure that it can successfully sell your program. Approximately 15 out of 100 programs submitted for review are accepted. But once your software is on the list, you will have an army of sales representatives putting your product on the shelves of hundreds of stores across the country.

Another drawback is the amount of money you will make. Naturally, everyone is in the business to make money and you must be willing to accept less than 100% of the list price on each sale because a percentage will go to the company that is distributing your software and another percentage will go to the store that sells it on your behalf.

In spite of the drawbacks, your product should get greater exposure than if you sold it yourself. This exposure should help sell more units but at a smaller profit margin. However, you stand to make as much or more money than if you sold your software by yourself primarily through mail-order advertising because most educators will want to have an opportunity to try out the program before they buy it. Having the program available for first-hand review will help sell your product at the point of sale if it's any good.

In addition, you will not have to worry about supporting an army of sales representives who go from store to store to sell and stock your product. The software distribution company will do all that for you.

CONTRACTING WITH MAJOR PUBLISHING COMPANIES

Many major educational publishers such as Harcourt Brace Jovanovich and Scott Foresman are starting divisions that produce educational software to accompany their materials.

ADVANTAGES

A teacher who is able to design and/or program educational software can find a niche with these companies on a contract basis. Begin by finding out what their software publishing agenda is. It will be to your advantage if you are already using that publisher's materials so you will have specific and practical suggestions on how the computer can be integrated with their materials. This will help the publisher sell more copies of your program to other teachers who also use their reading or math series.

This means that you work as an independent contractor on a project basis and are not considered a part of the regular staff. You may be paid a set amount for a specific project or on a royalty percentage based on net sales.

In addition, many educators are finding new career opportunities with these companies as part of the regular staff in jobs such as educational software developers, documentation writers (for the manuals that accompany the software programs), and educational technical editors. As a teacher who is a curriculum specialist and as one who knows principles of teaching and learning, your skills will be invaluable. It is not necessary to be a computer programmer to be able to develop or design educational software.

DISADVANTAGE

The publishing company may already have a lot of its work contracted out or already have staff on board.

EDUCATIONAL SOFTWARE PUBLISHING COMPANIES

As you browse through educational computer publications such as *Electronic Learning* or *Classroom Computer Learning,* you will notice ads soliciting educational software writers. Write to these companies to find out if they are interested in publishing your program(s).

The process of finding the right publisher is similar to that of finding a publisher for your book manuscript: (1) First, write a query letter to let them know that you have written a particular program and to find out if they are interested. If you're lucky and they are interested, (2) find out the conditions of publication (such as the royalty percentage, advances, documentation requirements, date the work is to be completed or submitted, and so on). When the contract arrives, be sure to consult your attorney regarding the fine points in the contract to make sure that your interests are protected. Royalties may vary, but 10% to 15% of net sales is a common figure.

ADVANTAGES

The publishing, marketing, and distribution are all done for you.

DISADVANTAGES

Your software is one of hundreds of titles so it may get lost in the shuffle.

RESOURCES

There are numerous resources for you to consult regarding writing, publishing, marketing, and selling educational software. Books such as *The Software Writer's Market* tell you what to write, whom to sell to, suggestions, and guidelines on how to write clear documentation. This volume contains thousands of company names and addresses with detailed listings showing (1) what programs publishers are looking for, (2) how they want you to submit your program, (3) how much they pay—and when. This volume is invaluable in that it will save you time in the process of finding the right publisher for your software. To order, write to IDF Publications, 146T Country Club Lane, Pomona, New York 10970, or call (914) 354-5585.

Organizations such as the Software Writers' International Guild (SWIG) enable educational software writers to keep up with the latest developments in the field. Organizations such as SWIG can often serve as your agent by representing you in a sale to software publishers, helping you develop your software, providing assemblers and utility programs, helping you locate companies and key individuals in the educational software field, offering local seminars and meetings, and providing legal services, job placement, and networking among members. (SWIG, P. O. Box 87, Stony Point, New York 10980, (914) 354-5585.)

REFERENCES

BAKER, F. T. (1972) "Chief programmer team management of production programming." IBM Systems J. 11 (January): 56-73.

BEEBE, T. H. (1983) "How to write your own instruction using a computer authoring system." Instructional Innovator (September): 34-35.

BLOOM, B. et al. (1962) Taxonomy of Educational Objectives. New York: Longman.

BOHL, M. (1980) "Information processing." SRA: Chapter 11.

BRACEY, G. W. (1982) "Computers in education: what the research shows." Electronic Learning (November/December).

BURKE, R. L. (1982) CAI Sourcebook: Background Procedures for Computer Assisted Instruction in Education and Industrial Training. Englewood Cliffs, NJ: Prentice-Hall.

BURKE, R. V. (1982) "If you're thinking about developing your own software, consider this . . . " Computers and Education (December): 12, 37.

COATES, B. (1982) "Curriculum development in CBL and the impact on teaching styles and methodology." Computers and Education 41.

DiGIAMMARINO, F., D. JOHNSON, and B. LOWD. (1982) Microcomputer Use and Software Design: From Start-Up Activities to Creating Software. Springfield, MA: Milton Bradley.

DOUGLASS, V. G. (1983) "CAI in the pocket." SR Software Rev. 2, 2: 73.

FISHER, G. (1983) "Where CAI is effective: a summary of the report." Electronic Learning (November/December): 82-84.

FRIEDMAN, D. (1983) "What is educational computing?" Educational Computer (November/December): 33.

GLEASON, G. T. (1981) "Microcomputers in education: the state of the art." Educational Technology (March): 11.

HANKANSSON, J. (1981) "How to evaluate educational courseware." J. of Courseware Rev. 1, 1.

HECK, W. P., J. JOHNSON, and R.J. KANSKY (1981) Guidelines for Evaluating Computerized Instructional Materials. National Council of Teachers of Mathematics.

KINGMAN, J. (1981) Designing good educational software." Creative Computing 7 (October).

KLEIMAN, G., M. M. HUMPHREY, and T. VAN BUSKIRK (1981) "Evaluating educational software." Creative Computing 7 (October).

KONTOS, G. (1984) "Authoring quality software for education." Computer Education (February).

LEWIS, R. (1983) "Teachers, pupils and microcomputers." Technological Horizons in Education J. (February): 31-32.

MECC Instructional Services (1980) "Guide to developing software for the Apple II." Presented at the AEDS/MACUL meeting, Winter.

PETERS, H. and J. JOHNSON (1978) "Author's guide: design development style packaging review." Conduit.

POPP, J. (1983) "The teachers computers will replace." Educational Computer (July/August): 24-35.

PRICE, R. V. (1982) "Selecting educational computer software." Educational Resources and
    Techniques (Spring/Summer): 5, 7.
PRICHARD, W. H., Jr. (1982) "Instructional computing in 2001: a scenario." Phi Delta Kappan
    63, 5: 322-325.
ROBLYER, M. D. (1983) "The case for and against teacher-developed microcomputer course-
    ware." Educational Technology (January): 14-17.
SPITLER, C. D., and V. CORGAN (1979) "Rules for authoring computer-assisted instruction
    programs." Educational Technology 14 (September).
STARKWEATHER, J. (1969) "A common language for a variety of programming needs," in
    Computer-Assisted Instruction—A Book Readings. New York: Academic Press.
WATSON, D. M. (1983) "A model for the production of CAL material." Computers and
    Education 7, 3.
WELDMAN, J. (1983) "The future of computers in education: what are the right questions?" T.
    H. E. Journal (September): 147-148.
WESTROM, M. (1977) "Summary and current status of NATAL-74." AEDS J. (Fall): 83-89.

ABOUT THE AUTHORS

Julie M. T. Chan, Ed. D., is the co-founder of Compukids Computer Learning Centers and Vice-President of Franchising and Marketing for the corporation. She is also a consultant for schools and systems setting up computer-based education programs, helping schools and districts plan, implement, and evaluate their computer programs. She writes, speaks, consults, and lectures internationally on computers in education. Chan is also the author of *Getting Your Child Off to a Good Start in Reading* and serves as the Reading Software Review Coordinator for the IRA publications, *The Reading Teacher* and *The Reading Journal*.

Marilyn Korostoff, M.A., is a middle school English and social studies teacher in Los Alamitos, California. She is also a part-time instructor at the University of California, Riverside, in the computer certificate program for educators. She has taught at the elementary, middle school, and university levels and specializes in the area of gifted education. Through her association with Dr. Julie Chan and Compukids, she became interested in computers and began teaching computer programming to both children and adults. Korostoff gives computer workshop presentations and has been involved in developing computer curriculum applications for classroom and staff development implementation.